UNBREAKABLE

Unbreakable: A 31 day Devotional on Overcoming Your Past and Taking Hold of Victory

Copyright © 2023 Leslie Warren

All rights reserved.
No part of this publication may be reproduced in a retrieval system, or transmitted in any form or by any means—electronic, mechanical, photocopying, recording, or otherwise—without the prior written permission of the publisher.

Scriptures taken from the Holy Bible, New International Version®, NIV®. Copyright © 1973, 1978, 1984, 2011 by Biblica, Inc.™ Used by permission of Zondervan. All rights reserved worldwide. www.zondervan.com The "NIV" and "New International Version" are trademarks registered in the United States Patent and Trademark Office by Biblica, Inc.™ Scripture quotations marked (NLT) are taken from the Holy Bible, New Living Translation, copyright ©1996, 2004, 2015 by Tyndale House Foundation. Used by permission of Tyndale House Publishers, Carol Stream, Illinois 60188. All rights reserved. Scripture quotations marked TPT are from The Passion Translation®. Copyright © 2017, 2018 by Passion & Fire Ministries, Inc. Used by permission. All rights reserved. ThePassionTranslation.com. All Scripture quotations are taken from THE MESSAGE, copyright © 1993, 2002, 2018 by Eugene H. Peterson. Used by permission of NavPress, represented by Tyndale House Publishers. All rights reserved. Scripture quotations taken from the Amplified® Bible (AMP), Copyright © 2015 by The Lockman Foundation. Used by permission. www.lockman.org. Scripture quotations marked CSB have been taken from the Christian Standard Bible®, Copyright © 2017 by Holman Bible Publishers. Used by permission. Christian Standard Bible® and CSB® are federally registered trademarks of Holman Bible Publishers. Scripture quotations taken from the Berean Study Bible, BSB, Copyright ©2016, 2020 by Bible Hub. Used by Permission. All Rights Reserved Worldwide. https://bereanbible.com.Scripture quotations marked (CEV) are from the Contemporary English Version Copyright © 1991, 1992, 1995 by American Bible Society. Used by Permission. Scripture quotations marked (PARA) are paraphrased versions of the original passage by the author, while maintaining fidelity to the original Hebrew, Greek, and Aramaic texts.

This manuscript has undergone viable editorial work and proofreading, yet human limitations may have resulted in minor grammatical or syntax-related errors remaining in the finished book. The understanding of the reader is requested in these cases. While precaution has been taken in the preparation of this book, the publisher and author assume no responsibility for errors or omissions, or for damages resulting from the use of the information contained herein.

Paperback ISBN: 9798390148273

A Publication of *Tall Pine Books*
119 E Center Street, Suite B4A | Warsaw, Indiana 46580
www.tallpinebooks.com

| 1 23 23 20 16 02 |

UNBREAKABLE

A 31 DAY DEVOTIONAL ON OVERCOMING YOUR PAST AND TAKING HOLD OF VICTORY

LESLIE WARREN

"If you are seeking encouragement and practical prayers to help you overcome challenges in this life, "Unbreakable" by Leslie Warren is a great devotional and resource. Leslie shares her faith journey and emphasizes the power of the Word of God while also giving a daily prayer to seal the truths she shares. Leslie describes an encounter with Jesus and the power of not only salvation but deliverance and full transformation. "Unbreakable" is an easy and relatable read. This also makes an excellent gift so go ahead and grab more than one because you are going to want to share it!"

–Lindsay Stone Corbett
Author of Gospel Glitter

*This book is in honor of the Praying Mamas
in my life whose fire for the things of God
sparked a hunger in me and taught me how
to go to battle in prayer. Their laid down lives
for Jesus continue to witness to me the power
of prayer and the love and kindness of God.*

*To my husband Greg-You have stood by me faithfully
through some of my greatest trials, and each time
I look at you I see the Father's unconditional love
displayed through you. I could not have written this
book without your love and continual support.
I love you always.*

*A special thank you to my friend Lora for speaking life
into my dream of writing a book, and for inspiring the
title of this devotional.*

*To my children-I pray that this book will serve as
a stone of remembrance for you that will help to
encourage and uplift you throughout life's storms and
always point you back to Jesus.*

CONTENTS

How To Use This Devotional.. *xiii*
Who is Depending on You?.. *xvii*
Let God Use your Story ....*xxiii*

1. Home 1
2. The Word 7
3. The God Who Answers By Fire 13
4. Unaware 19
5. Our Prize, Our Pleasure, Our Portion 25
6. Contentment is Free.. 29
7. Call to Me 33
8. Watch How I Do It 39
9. He's Afraid of Your Movement 45
10. Changed In His Presence 49
11. Unmet Expectations 53
12. He Said Regardless 57
13. Let Them Scatter 63
14. Don't Stop There... 69
15. There Will Be An "After" 73

16.	Heart Check	79
17.	Trust Me in the Fog	85
18.	Heaven's Angels	91
19.	What is Your Him?	97
20.	Comfort Zones	101
21.	Give Strife the Boot!	105
22.	Rejection Stings	109
23.	Make The Investment	119
24.	You've Been Built Into the Wall	125
25.	Stand Your Ground	129
26.	He's Still With You	133
27.	Let God Have A Turn	137
28.	Rise Up Warrior	141
29.	Do It Afraid	145
30.	Assumptions Can Be Costly	149
31.	Just One More Time	153
	About The Author	*161*
	Endnotes	*163*

HOW TO USE THIS DEVOTIONAL

I may not know the reason you picked up this book, but I am sure glad you did. It means you have your mind and heart made up that there is more for you than just living with your fears and regrets. You're going to need your Bible for this devotional as we dive into the Word of God and let the words renew our mind each day. I want you to open it up every day to the highlighted scripture for the day, and let it be your mediation for the day.

"This Book of the Law shall not depart from your mouth, but you shall read [and meditate

> *on] it day and night, so that you may be careful to do [everything] in accordance with all that is written in it; for then you will make your way prosperous, and then you will be successful." Joshua 1:8 AMP*

Secondly, I want you to find a place in your home, car, or another quiet place to let God speak to you as you read this devotional each day. This may be something you have to be intentional about if you have little ones at home or a challenging schedule. The goal is to get yourself in position to hear from God. Find what works for you. Each page has a unique story and point of view whether it be from my personal experiences or from the lives of people from the Bible. I share multiple encounters with God where He spoke to me through His Word, in prayer, and through visions. God also wants to speak directly into your life. He wants to draw you closer to Him throughout these 31 days and reveal to you His heart for your life.

Lastly, I want you to write your own story. I want the last few pages of this book to serve as a journal for you. I believe when we write out our stories we are actually laying it down through written words and giving it over to God to use it.

I'm not suggesting that God is asking you to write a book, but I am encouraging you to consider the ways God wants to use your story to share with others the power of God at work in your life. I resisted my story for many years because I was afraid of what people might think, say, or do. But I learned that God wanted to use my story to set others free. He wanted me to testify how He made me whole to encourage you today that He can do the same for you. I no longer look at my story the same. I don't see just the pain or rejection, but I see how God turned it around for good. He has used my story to bring about good in the lives of others and to reignite hope. I don't want you to be afraid of your story either. He is redeeming your story and mine and removing the very scent of the fire we have been through by replacing it with the sweet fragrance of Christ (2 Corinthians 2:15 AMP). Even the things we don't talk openly about. I won't go into too much detail here yet, but I am filled with joy for what God is planning to do in your life.

INTRODUCTION:
WHO IS DEPENDING ON YOU?

I don't know about you, but I sometimes feel completely overwhelmed by all that God has entrusted me with, all the promises He has spoken to accomplish and work through me. I think to myself, "Are You sure, God? Are You really sure I'm the one for this?" Feeling like you're just not enough, and someone better could do it instead, someone with more courage! Oh how real this was for me. Personally, I would have just rather stayed in my quiet place where I meet with Jesus with my Bible open and some instrumental worship playing in the background. The place where He speaks to the deep places of my heart, and He shows me His heart. During one of these times I was praying, I had a vision of myself on a beach with Jesus just resting, looking out into the ocean, and watching a beautiful sunset. I was feeling such peace just basking in His presence, and I didn't want to leave this spot! But then I turn around and see a multitude of people behind me, knowing I can't stay here forever, that I must go back out into my mission field for those faces I see that are depending on me. It causes me to reflect on James 2:17, "So too, faith, if it does not have works [to back it up], is by itself dead [inoperative and ineffective]" (AMP).

I've been blessed with a rich community of praying women, and one evening as we were all in one room praying, the Lord began to show me His heart for my life. We were all spread out across the room and as I was kneeling down on the outside, I was kicking and screaming inside my heart, saying, "Lord, I just don't want to! I can't do it! It's too hard! But Lord, don't let me leave You, don't let me give up!" I was being honest with Him about how insecure I felt about taking a step forward into unknown territory. He whispered to my heart, "Leslie, it's your legacy. Wouldn't you be upset if you paid for something from the store and it didn't do as it was created to do? Especially a really expensive item? You would do some form of grieving, get upset, and wonder why it would not work as it was created. You bought it because of its value to you.

You spent money on it because it meant something to you. Now envision how I must feel as your Creator. To have created you perfect in splendor and for you not to want to work, to be what I created you to be? After I paid such a high price for you. There are pieces in need of repair within you, but don't fret, for I know exactly where the repair is needed. I have all the tools to fix you back to my original intention for you. It won't take long, and as you work for Me and with Me, time will multiply. I will recover lost time. You'll work longer than any that have gone on this path before you and more efficiently than any other before you. The favor of the Lord is upon you." I remember pausing in wonder and in awe of what He was speaking to me. Then I began to hear more, "Would you even take the item back for not working? Not Me. I wait. I wait for the moment for you to give me permission to work on you and with you. Waiting for the day to see you do all I have intended for you to do. I can change parts of you but only you can power up, take from Me what you need, and choose to move." I sat still, listening intentionally as I didn't feel a release to speak or move. I began to hear these words of encouragement that I later shared with our prayer group: "Some of you think you're too old in age, but I've got fresh parts for you. Age cannot limit what I have for you. I will return to you a double portion in time back from what has been lost." My heart melted as I felt His love washing over me, because His Word says that He disciplines those He loves (Proverbs 3:12 NIV).

Oh how I did not understand the weight of this vision until I walked through some of the days I will share with you in this devotional. My prayer is that after reading this book, you see how precious you are in the eyes of God and step out into the unknown territory He may be calling you to, knowing that you don't step out alone.

These are scriptures I continue to draw strength from when my faith is being stretched, and I am walking with God into a new land:

Ephesians 3:20 AMP: *Now to Him who is able to [carry out His purpose and] do superabundantly more than all that we dare ask or think [infinitely beyond our greatest prayers, hopes, or dreams], according to His power that is at work within us....*

Isaiah 64:8 NIV: *Yet you, LORD, are our Father. We are the clay, you are the potter; we are all the work of your hand.*

Psalms 56:3 NIV: *When I am afraid, I put my trust in you.*

Exodus 4:11-12 AMP: *The Lord said to him, "Who has made man's mouth? Or who makes the mute or the deaf, or the seeing or the blind? Is it not I, the Lord? Now then go, and I, even I, will be with your mouth, and will teach you what you shall say."*

1 Peter 2: 9-10 MSG: *But you are the ones chosen by God, chosen for the high calling of priestly work, chosen to be a holy people, God's instruments to do his work and speak out for him, to tell others of the night-and-day difference he made for you—from nothing to something, from rejected to accepted.*

Philippians 2:13 AMP: *For it is [not your strength, but it is] God who is effectively at work in you, both to will and to work [that is, strengthening, energizing, and creating in you the longing and the ability to fulfill your purpose] for His good pleasure.*

PREFACE:
LET GOD USE YOUR STORY

In Luke 7, a story is told of a woman who began weeping at the feet of Jesus. As the tears poured over His feet, she began to wipe them with her hair. I see myself in the heart of this woman. A woman with a story to tell that wasn't picture perfect. A story we can assume based on what is mentioned about her is one of pain, rejection, and failure. She poured everything she was carrying at the feet of Jesus. Can you imagine? She didn't care who was looking at her. She didn't come to try and defend her story; she came to let God use it. Even though she was criticized for her actions, she never ceased to take her gaze off of the King of kings. Jesus quickly used her courageous actions to teach the crowd a lesson on forgiveness and unconditional love.

My story is not a neat and tidy one. It's messy. My story has moments of sadness and pain, embarrassment and rejection, but also forgiveness and redemption. God doesn't want us to hide from our story; He wants to use our story. My story speaks of a God who took a girl, broken and lost, and turned her life around and made her whole. I didn't have to hide anymore from my fears, regrets, and failures. I could unleash them through tears. Tears that spoke of my pain. My heart cried out, longing for acceptance and love. That's where I met Someone who knew me already, but I didn't yet even really know more than His name. His name was Jesus. He poured love into my heart that I remember only experiencing glimpses of as a child. I used to sing at church as a child, and I remember at times not being able to get through the song because I was overwhelmed with tears by the presence of God as I was worshiping His holy name. Not even quite understanding what it all fully meant at the time. But I won't go deep into the details of my story yet because the way I look at the moments of heartache in my life have changed, as I've seen the goodness and mercy of

God transform my life and redeem my story.

That's where the title of this book comes in. Unbreakable. Through all the pain and heartache in my life, it never broke me. I could've been a totally different person if it wasn't for Jesus. I would've drowned in my sorrows, but the Lord had been chasing after me all along. He had a story of redemption in the making for my life, and today I stand stronger and more confident than ever in God's power to transform a life and use it for His glory.

DAY 1:

HOME

So do not be ashamed to testify about our Lord or about me His prisoner, but with me take your share of suffering for the gospel [continue to preach regardless of the circumstances], in accordance with the power of God [for His power is invincible], 2 Timothy 1:8 AMP

I was a girl raised in church. My parents started off their marriage committed to raising their children in church. My Dad was called into ministry and became a pastor. We were at church every Sunday morning, sometimes Sunday night, and most definitely every Wednesday night. I remember that the most because I had friends who didn't go to a midweek service and I would complain about wanting to stay home and do other "fun" things like talk on the phone for hours with friends or watch television. I had a good upbringing. My Dad was a passionate preacher for the Lord. I remember him preaching the Word of God from the pulpit with such zeal that he would jump up and down at the altar while lifting up the Bible in his hand! I also sang in the choir as my Mom played the piano. I will never forget a song we used to sing often, and I would sing solo on the verses. It was called "Treasures Unseen." Every single time I would sing that song I could feel something tangible happening within my heart. A tugging within me. A few times as I was singing I burst out into tears and couldn't make it through. I remember running to the altar to give my heart to Jesus as a young girl. I had encounters with God at a very young age. I didn't have words for it all then, but now I see the evidence of His hand on my life all the while. I wish I could say that my relationship with the Lord grew from such a solid foundation, but my family later experienced the pain and devastation caused by sin in our home. Everything I knew was changing, including losing our family home and my Dad stepping down from his position as pastor of our church.

In 2007, I was blessed to be accepted into a college only three hours from home, and I moved in with a family member who lived in the area. I visited a few churches in the area, but God was not the center of my life at that time. I carried on trying not to focus on the worries at home, and instead focused on working, making good grades, and making new friends. Throughout that time God was connecting me with people that He was using to lead me back to Him. A special woman in particular became my sorority advisor and mentor, and she invited me to my current home church as a young adult. My very first visit to her church was with my college best friend on a Saturday night in 2012. What happened that night is hard to put into words. I had a tangible encounter with the presence of God during worship. Just like that little girl I told you about, singing "Treasures Unseen" from the pulpit, weeping in the presence of God. I repented of my sin, and for trying to live for myself and for the world. I confessed Jesus as my Lord and Savior. My heart had found its resting place in Him. I had returned home. I got plugged into that church, and the first ministry I became a part of was the choir. All I can say is, Wow, God! He restored my life. I am still amazed at God and how He orchestrated every detail. I was that prodigal child, lost in darkness, alone and afraid. Uncertain of who I was and where I was going. But I believe God was chasing after me, continuing to place people in my path that would point me to Him. This was only the beginning in my growing relationship with the Lord, and I cannot help but tell you of the goodness of God in my life!

A PRAYER FOR SALVATION

Heavenly Father, I believe in my heart that Jesus died on the cross of Calvary for me and for my sins. That You loved me so much that You sent Your Son to die for me. I believe with all my heart that Jesus was raised from the dead so that I could walk in freedom and be with You in heaven for all eternity. I humbly bow my heart before You in full surrender, and ask for Your forgiveness for my sins. I ask that You would come into my heart and be my Lord and Savior. I thank You Lord Jesus for laying down Your life for me, and I want to live for the rest of my days worshiping Your name and testifying with every breath I have of Your saving grace. You have made me whole and new! I have been washed and made clean by the blood of Jesus. Thank You for never giving up on me! Thank You for leading me home. Thank You for pulling me out of the pit, setting my feet on a solid rock, and giving me a firm place to stand! Glory to your name, Jesus! Amen. (Scripture references: Romans 10:9; 2 Corinthians 5:17; I John 1:7; Psalm 40:2)

THE LYRICS TO TREASURES UNSEEN BY ANN BALLARD[1]

My home may not look like a castle
And my clothes may be lacking in style.
And if you come sit at my table
A meager supply you might find.

God made a world filled with beauty
With things we enjoy everyday.
My secret to hidden possessions
Is to love Him and serve Him His way.

But Oh, it's not what you see
That makes me a King, makes me a King
To me, I've everything, all that I need
All that I need, treasures unseen.

DAY 2:

THE WORD

We demolish arguments and every pretension that sets itself up against the knowledge of God, and we take captive every thought to make it obedient to Christ. 2 Corinthians 10:5 NIV

I could spend hours talking to you about the Word of God, my friend. I've shared with you my story of how the blood of Jesus rescued me, but now I want to share with you how the Word of God freed my mind. I was on a journey with the Lord, but my mind was still very much in bondage. I needed God to re-shape my way of thinking because I was still very much uncertain of myself and who I was. I had to learn what God's Word says about me, and also recognize the thought patterns that spoke the opposite of that. I had to do what the Scriptures direct us to do—take every thought captive that is contrary to the Word of God and begin to replace it with His words.

I want to give you one very real example of this in action early on in my walk with Jesus. I was still learning about who I was in Christ from reading the Word of God, setting aside time daily to do this, and really just beginning to examine my thoughts more. I have notebooks full of revelation and knowledge the Lord would download into my Spirit each morning. I was hungry and on fire for God! I couldn't get enough of my time in His Word. But one thing was still present in my life. A fear that I had buried deep within my heart that I never really spoke about. It originated from a tragedy that happened to a very special person in my life. I looked up to this person as a role model, and they had made decisions that led them down a very dark path. The outcome in this situation was resolved, but the utter shock that it even happened was still rotating around in my mind. I thought that if it could happen to them, it could happen to me. I was tormented in this fear that something bad would happen to me, or that if I ever made a mistake, it could be costly and punishment would be due.

I could not make a single mistake without feeling like this impending doom was upon me. I also knew that I was flawed and that it was only a matter of time before I did something wrong. It was absolute torment. It started to impact my overall confidence and ability to do what I knew God called me to do. I became afraid of failure and it only increased my desire to achieve perfection. I held every mistake I made under a microscope, and it became huge to me. My husband didn't understand it at first. He just thought I was just striving to do well in all that I was given, but he soon realized that it was becoming obsessive. I was constantly going to him for validation. He would try to comfort me by talking it out with me, trying to get me to stop being so hard on myself, but fear would just return again. The fears I had were often very illogical when it came to something bad happening to me. It was clear I had taken ownership of these tormenting thoughts, and no matter what I tried, I couldn't shake them. Reasoning with the thought only provided a temporary solution, and ignoring it only increased the amount of time I was thinking about it.

I felt trapped, and it was only when I began declaring God's Word that I became free! I finally opened up to someone besides my husband about these thoughts. I shared them with a trusted friend and spiritual mentor who prayed with me and spoke over me a verse found in John 8:36: "So if the Son sets you free, you will be free indeed" (NIV). It was like when she declared it, I could feel the Lord making it personal to me. Something changed inside of me. I felt like I had something to grab hold of that would defeat this fear controlling my life! From that moment forward, I declared that scripture day in and day out. The thoughts did not go away suddenly, but I was faithful to read them, pray them, and even shout them! It became my lifeline, and it was as if I was sending God's Word out to fight for me! I began to realize that the devil, the enemy of our souls, had been attacking my mind and causing me to meditate on thoughts of fear, despair, and dread. I gave him notice when I picked up the Word of God as my sword (Ephesians 6:17 NIV)!

I started to declare more words of truth. I began to declare Jeremiah 29:11, that God's plans for me are good, and not for disaster, but to give me a future and a hope (NLT)! I grew more and more in revelation and knowledge of who I am in Christ, and that the blood of Jesus paid the price for my freedom. I became confident in my new identity as a daughter of God, and realized I was given authority over fear (Luke 10:19; 2 Timothy 1:7).

And then, one day I realized that the stronghold had been taken down in my mind. The fearful thoughts tormenting my mind were gone. It no longer had a hold on me. My friend, I am a living testimony that as you abide in His Word and embrace the truth, "it will release true freedom into your lives" (John 8:32 TPT). He is calling our thoughts to come up higher. To break agreement with the lies of the enemy, and come into agreement with His Word. I continue to apply this in all aspects of my life, no matter what I am facing. If I have a thought or emotion that contradicts God's Word, I SPEAK THE WORD! Fear can't stand. Anxiety can't stand. Depression can't stand. The Word of God prevails! When you know God's Word, you can learn to take thoughts captive that disguise themselves as truth.

PRAYER FOR TODAY

Lord Jesus, I thank You for the freedom that is in Your name. I thank You that not only did You die so that we could live forever in eternity with You, but that You came so that we could have life and life more abundantly right here on earth. I declare over my circumstances that Your name is above every name! It is above anxiety, depression, and fear!

I thank You that You have given us authority to take captive every thought to make it obedient to Christ. We break agreement with the lies of the enemy that bring confusion, fear, and unbelief (ask the Lord to reveal to you specifically some thoughts and beliefs that contradict His Word). We come into agreement with Your Word that says greater is He who is within me than he who is in the world. We come into agreement with Your Word that says we are a new creation in Christ Jesus, and who the Son sets free is free indeed. Your Word is powerful and sharper than any two-edged sword. You alone are my rock and my salvation, my fortress. I shall not be shaken. Your Word says that he who dwells in the shelter of the Most High will remain secure and rest in the shadow of the Almighty, whose power no enemy can withstand! Hallelujah! In Jesus' name I pray, Amen. (Scripture references: John 10:10; Philippians 2:9; 2 Corinthians 10:5; 1 John 4:4; 2 Corinthians 5:17; John 8:36; Psalm 62:6; Hebrews 4:12; Psalm 91:1)

DAY 3:
THE GOD WHO ANSWERS BY FIRE

Elijah went before the people and said, "How long will you waver between two opinions? If the Lord is God, follow him; but if Baal is God, follow him." But the people said nothing. Then Elijah said to them, "I am the only one of the Lord's prophets left, but Baal has four hundred and fifty prophets. Get two bulls for us. Let Baal's prophets choose one for themselves, and let them cut it into pieces and put it on the wood but not set fire to it. I will prepare the other bull and put it on the wood but not set fire to it. Then you call on the name of your god, and I will call on the name of the Lord. The god who answers by fire—he is God." 1 Kings 18:21-24 NIV

This story of Elijah's great faith in 1 Kings 18 has always amazed me! One man stood up against many, even his own people, and without wavering declared they have been deceived, and God is the ONLY real and true God! Even without having ever seen God face to face, he had enough experience with Him to side with God although his community was going down a different path. Elijah showed a boldness and courage that doesn't come from this world. Elijah could see that the minds of the Israelites were so clouded by the lies of the enemy that they had turned their hearts away from God and were captivated by false gods who could not help them. Elijah challenged the prophets of Baal and Asherah to call upon their gods to answer by fire and consume their sacrifices. To prove they were real. No matter what the prophets of these false gods did, their gods did not respond to them. They cried out and cried out, "Baal, answer us!" (v. 26 NIV). Then, it was Elijah's turn. Elijah repaired and rebuilt an old altar of the Lord that had been torn down, and placed his sacrifice on the wood. But then he took it one step further. He told them to pour water onto the offering and the trench surrounding the altar, until the area was totally consumed! Talk about God-confidence. He was confident God was going to show up. The Israelites stood still and watched as Elijah prayed to God saying, "Lord, the God of Abraham, Isaac and Israel, let it be known today that you are God in Israel and that I am your servant and have done all these things at your command. Answer me, Lord, answer me, so these people will know that you, Lord, are God, and that you are turning their hearts back again" (1 Kings 18:36-37 NIV). Suddenly, a fire fell upon the offering! It consumed the offering, the wood, the stones, the dust, and even the water in the trench! The Bible says that as the people were watching this miraculous event occur, "they fell prostrate and cried, "The Lord—he is God! The Lord—he is God!" (1 Kings 18:39 NIV).

As I read this story, I think of how far gone the Israelites had gotten away from God. I visualize a physical blinder over their eyes, causing them to be confused with a clouded mind. I see the altar that Elijah had placed his offering upon as a symbol of a clouded mind, watered down with confusion. God had proven himself faithful to the Israelites over and over, and yet their hearts turned away. I can relate to their apathy in my own life when I am not intentional about thinking on the faithfulness of God and meditating on His Word. He has proven that He is trustworthy, and yet I have turned to people, places, and things for help. In the end, I was left disappointed and often hurt. What I have learned is that if we aren't intentional about what we meditate on, our minds begin to drift away from what we were once confident in. We must anchor our minds in the Word of God. The enemy has been working overtime to water down our minds with lies of all types, attacking our insecurities, our fears, and tempting us with temporary pleasures. But thank God that no matter how clouded and confused your mind may be, God is the one true God who can touch your mind with His fire and consume every lie that is contrary to the truth!

ONE MORE THING

Elijah's offering was completely drowning in water and given the circumstances, it was impossible to set on fire. Maybe your mind is drowning today with thoughts of impossibilities, regret from your past mistakes, or your mind is consumed with worry about your future? Or maybe you've allowed the opinions of others to cause you to sway in your convictions? I thank God for the way of escape He has made for us! We can make a shift right now from confused to confident! We can repent and start naming the ways God has been good to us, and thanking Him for it! To come back to Him with a heart that remembers how He's been with us through the darkest times. You will soon find yourself praising God and experiencing the joy and peace that is found in knowing Him. When we confess our sins with a repentant heart He removes our shame (1 John 1:9 AMP). The Lord understands our struggles, and He isn't afraid of our emotions. He encourages us to bring them to Him! He knows me better than anyone, flaws and all, and still has been the best friend I have ever had. He has never walked away from me, no matter what I've done, and I can say with confidence He is not walking away from you either.

DAY 4:
UNAWARE

He entered into the world he created, yet the world was unaware. He came to the people he created—to those who should have received him, but they did not recognize him. But those who embraced him and took hold of his name he gave authority to become the children of God! John 1:10-12 TPT

Unaware. I was struck by those words on the page. That the Son of God came to earth to save all those who would put their trust in him, and yet many were unaware. It takes me to Nathanael's encounter in John 1, who speaks of the God who SEES!

The next day, Jesus decided to go to Galilee,

where he found Philip. Jesus said to him, "Come and follow me." (Now Philip, Andrew, and Peter had all grown up together in the village of Bethsaida.) Philip went to look for his friend, Nathanael, and told him, "We've found him! We've found the One we've been waiting for! It's Jesus, son of Joseph from Nazareth! He's the One whom Moses and the prophets prophesied would come!" Nathanael sneered, "Nazareth! What good thing could ever come from Nazareth?" Philip answered, "Come and let's find out!" When Jesus saw Nathanael approaching, he said, "Here comes a true son of Israel—an honest man with no hidden motive!" Nathanael was stunned and said, "But you've never met me—how do you know anything about me?" Jesus answered, "Nathanael, right before Philip came to you, I saw you sitting under the shade of a fig tree." Nathanael blurted out, "Teacher, you are truly the Son of God and the King of Israel!" Jesus answered, "Do you believe simply because I told you I saw you sitting under a fig tree? You will experience even more impressive things than that! I prophesy to you eternal truth: From now on, you all will see an open heaven and gaze upon the Son of Man like a stairway reaching into the sky with the messengers of God climbing up and down upon him!" (John 1:43-51 TPT)

According to the *Enduring Word Commentary* on Jesus' words, "I saw you," "It is possible Nathanael liked to pray and meditate upon God and His Word under the shade of an actual fig tree. Yet, under the fig tree was a phrase Rabbis used to describe meditation on the Scriptures. We can suppose that Nathanael spent time in prayer and in meditating on the Scriptures, and Jesus told him "I saw you" there."[8]

When Jesus says that He saw Nathanael "under the fig tree" it's a possibility that it actually references a place or posture of prayer! So Jesus was actually saying to him, "I saw you in your sacred place of prayer!" When Jesus made this comment, Nathanael's reaction shows that it was a very personal and intimate place and time for him! That only God would have known about. Nathanael blurts out, "Teacher! It's you!" Do you have a sacred place in your life, or places, that you've gone to pray and you remember specific encounters with God there? Or maybe in your prayer time you've wondered if God has even heard you? Where you poured it all out with words, tears, or groanings coming up from your spirit? It becomes a sacred place where you've emptied out your heart and poured out all the pain. Living in this harsh world, maybe you've had several of these moments like me. Believe that because God saw Nathanael, He also sees you travailing in prayer hoping against all hope, standing on a promise from God weeping for your health, your finances, your loved ones, our country, the world! He's saying, "I see you!" I also believe He is saying I want you to believe Me for GREATER! Even when the situation doesn't look the way you thought it would today. Nathanael didn't believe anything good could come from Nazareth, but that was exactly where his answer was coming from.

What if He's calling us to get back on the altar of surrender, and pray again for those things we've given up on? The things we don't see working out like we thought they would, but we have a word from GOD! My prayer is to also be a friend like Philip was to Nathanael. He came for Nathanael and wanted him to SEE what He saw! The passage tells us they had both been praying and waiting for the Messiah, and Philip comes with excitement, declaring "He's HERE!" I want to be an encouragement to my sisters in Christ who are feeling unseen and unheard, and remind them that He is right there with them, His attention is toward them, and He is listening. Although you may feel unaware of Him at times, He is very aware of you. Let's go to Jesus together in prayer, arm in arm! Come and see!

ONE MORE THING

I love that Jesus says to him, "Nathanael, *right before* Philip came to you I saw you sitting under the fig tree." Can you imagine the answer to your prayer coming as close as the very end of your AMEN? As Nathanael was praying, the answer was already coming toward him. The answer was on the way! I see prayer like this, a candle on a window seal, lit continually, believing and trusting in what God has promised. It's as if the light is there to welcome the promise in. To say, "Here, it's this house! It's me!" A hopeful expectation of good, because God is good. His ways are perfect. That candle says I'm waiting expectantly for the promise to arrive at any moment. Isn't that faith? Isn't that prayer? His promises are His goodness coming toward us, even now.

DAY 5:
OUR PRIZE, OUR PLEASURE, OUR PORTION

Yahweh, you alone are my inheritance. You are my prize, my pleasure, and my portion. You hold my destiny and its timing in your hands. Your pleasant path leads me to pleasant places. I'm overwhelmed by the privileges that come with following you! Psalm 16:5 TPT

Studying Psalm 16 has transformed my thinking from what it means to "enjoy the fullness of my salvation" as it talks about in Psalm 91:16 (TPT). Psalm 16 says that Jesus is our prize, our pleasure, and our portion. There is nothing we have need of that can't be found in Him. This anchors us in contentment. He is our prize, and everything else is His goodness in our lives. His goodness is our family, our home, our job, our ministry, etc. What better friend would or could be there with you through everything you face! Not only is He our prize, but we are His (John 3:16).

I wanted to go even deeper in this revelation of Jesus as our portion. According to *The New Strong's Concordance*, the Hebrew word for "portion" is *manah,* as it describes something weighed out (Strong 1996, 1052). This tells me that weighed out next to everything in our lives, Jesus is the prize, our pleasure, and our portion. I've weighed it out against everything else in my life (people, places, things), and nothing compares to Him. Even in my wandering, He's proven that He is present and faithful. Jesus is the center of my heart, and I've learned to cling to His every Word like an anchor in a storm.

My friend, not only is He your prize, but His promises are His goodness coming toward you. Psalm 23:6 says, "Surely your goodness and mercy shall follow me all the days of my life" (NIV). According to *The New Strong's Concordance*, the word "follow" in Hebrew is *radaph*, which means to run after, to pursue, to chase (Strong 1996, 458). We are being chased down by His goodness everyday! As

I began to meditate on these things, I began to realize that what was weighing down my heart was rooted in a wrong focus. I was searching for meaning in my roles, my relationships, my status, my possessions, and continued to come up empty and wanting more. But as I recalibrated my focus on my prize being all that I already have in Jesus, I stopped trying to hold it all together. I felt free of the heavy weight of expectations and started to "enjoy the fullness of my salvation."

PRAYER FOR TODAY

Lord Jesus, You are my prize, my pleasure, and my portion. I desire to be in Your presence more than anywhere else. My heart is full of thankfulness for all You have done for me, and Your constant mercy and protection over my life. Thank You for the contentment that comes from knowing You. There is nothing that compares to You. In Your name I pray, Amen.

> *For here is what the Lord has spoken to me: "Because you loved me, delighted in me, and have been loyal to my name, I will greatly protect you. I will answer your cry for help every time you pray, and you will feel my presence in your time of trouble. I will deliver*

you and bring you honor. I will satisfy you with a full life and with all that I do for you. For you will enjoy the fullness of my salvation!" Psalms 91:14-16 TPT

DAY 6:
CONTENTMENT IS FREE

In every situation [no matter what the circumstances] be thankful and continually give thanks to God; for this is the will of God for you in Christ Jesus. 1 Thessalonians 5:18 AMP

At the end of the holiday season in the year 2022, I had determined I was going to seek God and truly bask in the wonder of our savior's birth. During a time of prayer and intercession for a need close to my heart, the words "contentment is free" came to my mind. At first I didn't really understand that statement other than on the surface, but then I heard, "There's a redeeming story in the works for that." I knew it was the Holy Spirit speaking directly to the need I had been praying about, which included healing in relationships. He was encouraging me to hold on to hope, be thankful, don't cast away your confidence, the story is not over. In my own life it has been true that if I am content, I feel more at ease in my mind, peaceful, and generally more thankful. Not from my situation being 100% solved, but from placing my trust in God. Putting my trust in God is enough. I speak that truth over those thoughts that tell me I'm not doing enough to solve the problem, and that I should feel the weight of the burden on my shoulders. No. My Father says to bring my heavy burdens to Him, and the same is true for you (Psalm 55: 22 PARA). I feel more at rest not because I'm satisfied with what I see, but because nothing is impossible with God. I can't let the enemy rob me of my joy and tempt me towards control.

You know how it goes in our human minds when we think of something not working, it's hard to see what is. As I was in and out of sleep one night, I saw people and situations in my life swirling around in my head and every time I heard those hopeful words, "I have a story of redemption for that"..... over and over with each face, name, and problem.

According to *Merriam-Webster Dictionary,* the word "redeeming" means serving to offset or compensate for a defect.[5] He's making the wrong things right. He can redeem anyone's story. No cause too hopeless. His hand is not too short that He can't reach down and touch our needs *and* He *wants* to (Isaiah 59:1 NIV)! I can be thankful in every situation because I know in the end God will turn it around for good. He told me to imagine what that situation would look like: healed, restored, and made new? We've got to get in agreement with God! Join me in being thankful for what's working and trusting God with what isn't. Receive the peace He's wanting to give us. There is a story in the making, and it's not the end until it's good!

PRAYER FOR TODAY

I pray that as you read this you feel the very nearness of God in your midst, and that you become even more and more aware that you are seen and loved by Him! I pray He will replace any weariness with His peace and courage that causes us to tread upon even greater heights of grace and glory with our Beloved! If you've felt the wind knocked out of you this week, I pray you find peace and hope in knowing that though the righteous fall seven times, we RISE again! God's got you and everything that concerns you! (Scripture references: Habakkuk 3:19 NIV; Proverbs 24:16 AMP; Psalm 138:8 AMP)

DAY 7:
CALL TO ME

'Call to Me and I will answer you, and tell you [and even show you] great and mighty things, [things which have been confined and hidden], which you do not know and understand and cannot distinguish.' Jeremiah 33:3 AMP

Jeremiah 33:3 is one of those verses that you can meditate on every single day and still learn more about our loving Father. It says we can call out to God, and He will answer us. In Psalm 27:8, it says God also calls out to us to come (TPT)! A young Samuel heard the voice of the Lord calling out to him.

Then the Lord came and stood and called as at the previous times, "Samuel! Samuel!" Then Samuel answered, "Speak, for Your servant is listening." 1 Samuel 3:10 AMP

We can call to Him day or night, but He also calls out to His children! One day this verse began to take on new meaning in my life. I began to hear a calling to come closer to Him. It wasn't an audible voice, but it was a stirring within me that I couldn't shake. As I began to feel this drawing to come and talk with Him, I also began to pour out words that were hidden within my heart. I just started to speak and words began to flow. Honesty about my disappointments and failures began to pour out of my heart and I felt a weight lift off of me. Isn't it true that we often try to hide our pain instead of laying it down at the feet of Jesus so we can be free? I was led to Psalm 27:10 where David says, "My father and mother abandoned me, But you, Yahweh, took me in and made me Yours" (TPT).

The Father was reminding me that He hadn't abandoned me in my pain. Even the pain that I had caused to myself. His love was healing me of my shame, and reminding me of His commitment to me as His daughter. He will be faithful to complete the good work He started within us (Philipphians

1:6 PARA). He doesn't hide in silence from you out of embarrassment. In 1 Corinthians 13:7, it says that love bears all things and endures all things (AMP). Maybe we can't even imagine that kind of love because of the hurt we've experienced in relationships. I am here to remind myself and you today that we can come out of hiding. Shame and guilt are often the chains that keep us from coming toward our Father. There is forgiveness and grace in the arms of the Father. His arms are the safest place you can be. It is a place free from the accusations of the enemy. I picture myself climbing up into His giant lap, with eyes filled with tears, as He holds me close. The Father is waiting for the moment when we answer His call to come when we are ashamed, afraid, or hurting. When we come and spend time with Him, we become more acquainted with His nature and learn of His ways. We become transformed from the inside out. He is not looking for perfection, He is looking for your commitment.

> *I heard your voice in my heart say, "Come, seek my face;" my inner being responded, "Yahweh, I'm seeking your face with all my heart."* Psalm 27:8 TPT

ONE MORE THING

In the summer of 2022, I felt impressed to pick up this ugly cracked seashell on the beach on our family vacation. I've carried it with me ever since! It reminds me of God's love for me, scars and all. Past and all. He doesn't walk down the beach looking for the most perfect shells like we do. He looks for the ones that don't quite yet know and understand their beauty, until the Father's hand reaches down and picks them up. The ones that have a story to tell. You instantly feel known, loved and whole! I don't want to ever leave that place of being in awe that He chooses me. He chose you! He doesn't just put up with you, He takes delight in you (Zephaniah 3:17 NIV)! Wow!!! I could just burst knowing that.

This is a declaration that I pray often, and it comes from Jeremiah 33:3, Philippians 3:3, and Matthew 5:48:

> Heavenly Father, Your Word says that I can call to You and You will answer me, and tell me and even show me great and mighty things that I do not know and understand. Placing no confidence in who I am in the flesh, but confidence and focus in the perfection of You and who You are! Thank You for the work You are doing

within me, that I am growing into spiritual maturity both in mind and character. In Jesus Name I Pray, Amen.

DAY 8:
WATCH HOW I DO IT

Come to Me, all who are weary and heavily burdened [by religious rituals that provide no peace], and I will give you rest [refreshing your souls with salvation]. Take My yoke upon you and learn from Me [following Me as My disciple], for I am gentle and humble in heart, and you will find rest (renewal, blessed quiet) for your souls. For My yoke is easy [to bear] and My burden is light. Matthew 11:28-30 AMP

The Message: The Bible in Contemporary Language, conveys the text of Matthew 11:28-30 like this: "Are you tired? Worn out? Burned out on religion?

Come to me. Get away with me and you'll recover your life. I'll show you how to take a real rest. Walk with me and work with me—watch how I do it. Learn the unforced rhythms of grace. I won't lay anything heavy or ill-fitting on you. Keep company with me and you'll learn to live freely and lightly." We've all probably heard this scripture a time or two, but what hit me were the words "watch how I do it." As I read this, the Holy Spirit began to reveal to me that I had made agreement with a lie from the enemy. I had heard it before. In fact, my spiritual mother in the Lord had exposed this lie to a group of us during a prayer retreat. It was the phrase, "It's all up to me." The Lord began to reveal what was hidden within my own heart and showed me that I had believed this lie for quite some time. It was as if He was saying, "Leslie, you are looking at this situation from your perspective, trying to figure out all the answers, and make the best possible outcome happen." He revealed that I had been heavily burdened by a religious mindset that provided no peace. A religious mindset tells us that the What, the Who, the How, and the When is *us*. It's a focus on our works and performance, striving to do it all ourselves, with pressure that the end result is up to us. Then we catch a glimpse of our faults, failures, and fears, and give up before we ever get started. This mindset keeps us from coming to God like the scripture commands.

But my turning point came when I grasped hold of the truth that God is the What, the Who, the How, and the When! "God said to Moses, 'I AM WHO I AM'; and He said, 'You shall say this to the Israelites, 'I AM has sent me to you'" (Exodus 3:14 AMP). There is nothing that I face that would not fit under this umbrella. The Great I AM is the HOW for my child, the WHAT for my finances, the WHO for my weariness, and the WHEN for my breakthrough. It's not all up to me! He is the Waymaker! As this lie was exposed, I felt the grip of pressure to do it all....release! I felt the peace of God, and my faith increased for what God can do through me and in my situation.

Would you give Him access to the hidden places within your own heart so that He can begin to uncover the lies of the enemy that have held you captive and stolen your peace? My weariness left me, and I began to feel joy again! The burden was released, and I started to pick up hope again, knowing that God is in control and nothing is too hard for Him. I didn't need to fix anything. I just needed to surrender it to God. The One who made the sun, the moon, and the stars with a spoken word (Genesis 1). If that wasn't hard for Him, then we can rest assured that whatever we encounter in this life isn't going to scare Him away either.

> *...for I know Him [and I am personally acquainted with Him] whom I have believed [with absolute trust and confidence in Him and in the truth of His deity], and I am persuaded [beyond any doubt] that He is able to guard that which I have entrusted to Him until that day [when I stand before Him].* 2 Timothy 1:12 AMP

PRAYER FOR TODAY

Lord Jesus, my anxiety and overwhelming emotions are showing me that I'm not fully grasping Your love today. I'm not fully grasping all that You've given me because You love me. So instead of letting my emotions lead me into fear and confusion, I choose to believe that I have access to peace that transcends all understanding and that no situation can pluck me out of Your hands. I am reminded of the history in our relationship, and that You have never failed me. Not even once. I thank You Lord that no matter what it looks like, You are in control of it all. I place my confidence in what You can do because I remember all that You've already done. I thank You that You care about every single detail of my life, and that I can feel Your wrap-around presence in each moment. I can rest in knowing that You've gone into my tomorrow and made a way where there was no way before. I hear You singing over me and giving me a new song in my heart. I see You taking hold of my hand, with a warm smile on Your face, saying, "Be still, and know that I am God." (Scripture references: Philippians 4:7 AMP; John 10:28 AMP; Psalm 16:8 TPT; Zephaniah 3:17 NIV; Psalm 46:10 NIV)

> *For the mountains may be removed and the hills may shake, But My lovingkindness will not be removed from you, Nor will My covenant of peace be shaken," Says the LORD who has compassion on you.* Isaiah 54:10 AMP

DAY 9:
HE'S AFRAID OF YOUR MOVEMENT

Take My yoke upon you and learn from Me [following Me as My disciple], for I am gentle and humble in heart, and you will find rest (renewal, blessed quiet) for your souls. Matthew 11:29 AMP

Why is the enemy so desperate to stop us, that he plants a lie in our minds to get us to agree with him about ourselves, about others, about our situation? It's because he's afraid of our movement. He's so desperate to freeze us before we ever begin. When we come to the Lord, we begin to move with Him in His power and might, to accomplish all that our Father has purposed for our lives.

Going back to Matthew 11:29. *Enduring Word Commentary* invites us to look at this scripture in a different way. "The yoke is easy and the burden is light because He bears it with us. Borne alone, it might be unbearable; but with Jesus it can be easy and light. When training a new animal (such as an ox) to plow, ancient farmers often yoked it to an older, stronger, more experienced animal who bore the burden and guided the young animal through the learning process."[6] These words leaped off the screen as I read them. The enemy is afraid of our movement because he's afraid of WHO we are yoked with! We are yoked with Jesus Christ! It's not all up to us like the enemy would have us believe. It's not up to me to carry the weight of the world. It's not all up to me to save my family. It's not all up to me to see that relationship restored. Jesus is the stronger and more experienced One we are yoked with, and He bore our burdens and continues to guide and teach us. We cannot do anything in and of ourselves, but when we are yoked with Jesus we can do all things through Him who gives us strength (Philippians 4:13 AMP)!

ONE MORE THING

I have a very talented friend who can make the most beautiful flower arrangements and often can create something from nothing and make it into a beautiful centerpiece that lights up a room. She has actively used her gift of creativity for many years, and her talent has just increased. She shared with me that although many have expressed their appreciation and love for her servant's heart, her talent has often caused jealousy in beloved relationships. She took this heartache to God and laid it at His feet, and He began to reveal to her that her talent had continued to grow and she was able to do even more because she used what God had given her. I thought of the scripture that says, "For to everyone who has, more will be given, and he will have more than enough..." (Matthew 25:29 HCSB). I want to use what God has given me, don't you? I feel a sense of urgency that we must walk in obedience if we want to see miracles take place in our lives and in the lives of those we love. We step out in obedience, and God is in charge of the results.

DAY 10:
CHANGED IN HIS PRESENCE

My flesh and my heart may fail, But God is the rock and strength of my heart and my portion forever. Psalm 73:26 (AMP)

Psalm 73 caught my attention by the complete transparency of the author about his feelings. From the start, you can discern he is about to tell us of a challenging time in his life when "my feet came close to stumbling" (v. 2). He shares his frustrations in seeing the wicked prosper in their ways, and they do not seem to have a care in the world about their sinful behaviors. The psalmist describes the people appearing to be at ease in their lives, and their wealth continued to increase (v. 12).They did not fear God, even saying, "How does God know? Is there knowledge [of us] with the Most High?" (v. 11). The psalmist was even tempted to speak out his feelings of frustration against them (v. 15). He had allowed what was happening on the outside to affect him on the inside. Although he tried to make sense of it all, he eventually determined it was too great for his limited understanding and caused him pain to do so (v. 16). But then a shift happens, and he describes an encounter with the Lord that changed his perspective. He was awakened to the truth of what he had that they did not. He knew the One who had the final say. The wicked may appear to be prospering today, but it is only temporary. If they didn't get their hearts right with God, they would perish along with all they had gained from this world (v. 27).

I find encouragement in his invitation to come into the sanctuary of God with every kind of emotion that is also causing us a great deal of pain and heaviness. It wasn't until the author came to God that he received understanding and release from his burdens. It reminds me that God cares about what concerns us. God desires to clear pathways in our minds of wrong thinking and create new pathways of right thinking that are in alignment with Him. The author was very much focused on the negative around him, that he couldn't see or hear where God was in the midst of the situation. It appeared as if evil was prevailing against good. The author's perspective of the situation caused him to grow cold and weary, saying his "heart was embittered, and I was pierced within" (v. 21). But when he came into the presence of God just as he was, he was given a new strength. The psalmist began to see an abundance of reasons to be thankful, and a greater trust and reliance on God was set in his heart. Even as the author was tossing and turning in his emotions, he was reminded that "nevertheless I am continually with you, you have taken hold of my right hand" (v. 23). His current state of emotions didn't have to be a permanent destination. I'm thankful to know that I don't have to rely on my own understanding and have the answers to all my questions. I'm thankful that I can say "nevertheless" about what is happening around me or on the inside of me, and know that God never pulls away from me and He welcomes me into His presence where I find rest. The psalmist declares, "My flesh and my heart may fail, But God is the strength of my heart and my portion forever" (v. 26).

PRAYER FOR TODAY

Father, I come to You with a heart filled with questions and concerns about the evil I see prospering in our world. I come into Your sanctuary to surrender all the cares for the unknowns surrounding me. I can't carry this burden alone. Deliver me from the temptation to meditate on fear, focus on the negative, and be watchful for the bad to come. Help me to focus on Your Word that promises protection, peace, and Your presence no matter what is going on in the world around me. I lay my questions and insecurities at Your feet, Jesus. It's too great a burden to bear. It's a stumbling block that's keeping me from walking in Your perfect peace. Let me not grow weary and lose heart. Lord, empower me by Your Spirit. Renew my hope in You. You are my ever-present help in time of need. In Your Name I Pray, Amen. (Scripture references: Isaiah 26:3; Hebrews 12:1-3; Isaiah 40:31; Psalm 46:1)

> *But those who wait for the Lord [who expect, look for, and hope in Him] Will gain new strength and renew their power; They will lift up their wings [and rise up close to God] like eagles [rising toward the sun]; They will run and not become weary, They will walk and not grow tired.* Isaiah 40:31 AMP

DAY 11:
UNMET EXPECTATIONS

For in Him our heart rejoices, Because we trust [lean on, rely on, and are confident] in His holy name. Psalms 33:21 AMP

"In Him our heart rejoices" is what the psalmist writes as he praises the Lord and encourages us to rejoice in His faithfulness. As I was reading this scripture I didn't feel like much rejoicing was even possible. I was currently in a season of disappointment that I couldn't seem to shake. I desperately wanted to see healing take place in a close relationship in my life, and despite my best efforts, it just wasn't working. What do we do when we find ourselves trying to make sense of it all? I did what I had learned to do throughout my history with Jesus. Go to the Word of God and to my place of prayer. I got under my fig tree, like Nathanael did, and I laid it all out before the Lord. He began to show me a fresh perspective about expectations. I had been so focused on the one relationship that wasn't changing instead of seeing all the relationships that were flourishing. I began to see more clearly that I had been so focused on the negative that my emotions eventually caught up and joined my pity party. That's truly what it was, me feeling sorry for myself. In the Lord's goodness and mercy, He wasn't going to just leave me in my suffering. He came to rescue me, and reminded me that He has not forgotten me and was right there with me. He saw how the enemy planted one thought of discouragement in my mind that I grabbed hold of and ran with it! I had stepped out of faith and stepped into worry and disappointment that this beloved relationship would never be restored. I needed to break out. I needed to praise God and be thankful for what is working (relationships, provision, health, etc.), and trust God with what is not working. That was my role in it all. He was calling me to rest and to rejoice in His faithfulness.

In Luke 7:1-9, it talks about a Roman officer who

didn't get caught up in expectations. He didn't limit God but believed that Jesus could not only touch his servant and heal him, but He could just SPEAK the word and healing would flow. And it did! He wasn't setting the expectation of how Jesus would heal, but because he understood authority, it unlocked his miracle. Jesus has the authority to heal, restore, and make new. This man was even outside of the Jewish community, and Jesus marveled at his faith!

I didn't know how God was going to restore the relationship in my life, but I just knew that He had a story of redemption in the making. I could make the choice to keep on trusting and believing that God was in the middle of my situation. I could choose to receive and rest in His peace and trust His timing. He has never failed me, and my heart knows He never will.

ONE MORE THING

Don't abandon the plan because it doesn't look like you thought it would. The plan is still good because God is still good! I'm declaring it from my heart, over every promise He's given. He is still good! Every promise from His word is still good and true! His promise is the plan. We have no plan B. We look to Him, and we will surely not be disappointed!

I would have despaired had I not believed that I would see the goodness of the LORD In the land of the living. Wait for and confidently expect the LORD; Be strong and let your heart take courage; Yes, wait for and confidently expect the LORD. Psalms 27:13-14 AMP

DAY 12:
HE SAID REGARDLESS

Not that I speak from [any personal] need, for I have learned to be content [and self-sufficient through Christ, satisfied to the point where I am not disturbed or uneasy] regardless of my circumstances. Philippians 4:11 AMP

Becoming a new mom I quickly realized that quiet time alone with my thoughts and in prayer wouldn't happen unintentionally. I had to set aside time to get quiet before the Lord, and to ask my husband for help. He gladly would take over, and I would either go into my prayer closet, or take a warm shower. On one particular day I had my music set to play from my playlist while in the shower, but for some reason the water didn't stay hot; it turned cold quickly. Then, out of all of the songs on my playlist an old school classic rock song came on. I remember feeling so upset because I just wanted to fix my thoughts on Jesus and hear worship music that spoke the Word of God through song! I knew that was just what my heart needed so I blurted out in frustration, "Lord, I'm just trying to get into Your presence and hear Your voice and now look! But God I know You can change the song and change the water back to hot!" It must've been a stressful day to say the least! Nevertheless, God met me there and I will never forget the deep sense of conviction I felt in my heart in that moment of stillness and raw emotions. You see, I was looking for the atmosphere to be right before I felt that I could get into the presence of God. I had been waiting for that quiet moment all day, and God was saying to me that He is not just in the quiet; he's in my chaos too. He had been there all along. He's present, and no matter what was going on around me, I could always reach out to Him. I just needed to call out to Him.

That afternoon I started to think about how my to-do list got in the way of the simplicity of just being with Jesus "in the midst" of what's going on around me. I began to understand how I had allowed my emotions to dictate the way I interacted with God. Did I really need things to be different in my circumstances for me to have a restful heart? I took my question to the Word of God and ended up reading the words of Paul as he wrote "regardless" of the circumstances, I am content in the Lord (Philippians 4:11 Berean Standard Bible).

During an extended time of prayer, I received a vision and heard the word "banquet." I began to press into this, and this verse jumped off the page from the parable of the marriage feast: "But they paid no attention [they disregarded the invitation, treating it with contempt] and went away, one to his farm, another to his business" (Matthew 22:5 AMP). I saw myself in the vision sitting down at an empty wooden table looking down, and as I would look up slightly I could see a banquet table across from me that was full of food representing all the provisions I could ever need. The Lord began to show me that the voices of fear, unbelief, and love of self had led me to this empty table. He said that I move from the empty table to the banquet table depending on my circumstances. If my circumstances look dim, I move back over to the empty table in disappointment, dread, and fear. When everything seems to be falling into place, I'm back at the banquet table full of faith! (I could definitely see how this had played out in my emotions!) The challenge is this—who or what am I paying more attention to than the promises of God? Have I ignored countless invitations into His presence for the love of self or other things? You can imagine the conviction and repentance of my heart after He revealed this to me, but it was the hard truth that was keeping me from enjoying my inheritance as a daughter of God.

The Bible encourages us in 1 Thessalonians 5:18 to "give thanks in all circumstances; for this is God's will for you in Christ Jesus" (NIV). It wasn't my circumstances that needed changing; it was the posture of my heart. Set up an altar from the depths of your heart today, and kneel down before Him. Even if you hear clanging toys in the background of kids playing, or a dog barking, or the phone ringing. Set your gaze on Him. We don't need our circumstances to change to "feel" joy. We live from joy. The joy of the Lord is our strength (Nehemiah 8:10). He is all we need. He always has been. He always will be.

ONE MORE THING

Delay is not rejection. God has not rejected us, or rejected our prayers, or changed His mind and turned against His Word. People may have made promises to you and didn't keep them, but that will never be so with God! God is not a man, that He should lie. He is faithful to do just as He said! I pray that it gives you comfort today to keep praying and trusting. He loves you so much and has not forsaken you! (Scripture reference: Numbers 23:19 AMP)

> *And will not [our just] God defend and avenge His elect [His chosen ones] who cry out to Him day and night? Will He delay [in providing justice] on their behalf? I tell you that He will defend and avenge them quickly. However, when the Son of Man comes, will He find [this kind of persistent] faith on the earth?* Luke 18:7-8 AMP

DAY 13:
LET THEM SCATTER

Now Saul waited seven days, according to the appointed time which Samuel had set, but Samuel had not come to Gilgal; and the people were scattering away from Saul. 1 Samuel 13:8 AMP

Have you ever wondered what happened to King Saul in the Bible? How did he go from God's chosen and anointed King for Israel to a man no longer concerned with pleasing God. I want to explore this story a bit with you in hopes that we can find greater wisdom for our own lives and callings. In the beginning we see Samuel anointing Saul with oil, and shortly afterwards the Spirit of the Lord came upon

Saul, and he began to prophesy! He was a changed man, just as Samuel said he would be, and he became unrecognizable by those who knew him previously (1 Samuel 10:1, 6, 10-11 PARA). God indeed called him and chose him to be set apart for a great purpose!

Where was the turning point? Let's dig further into the unfolding of his story. In 1 Samuel 13, we see Saul and the Israelites facing a battle with the Philistine army. Samuel said he would come to Saul at Gilgal and instructed Saul to wait seven days until he came to him, and they would offer the burnt offerings and peace offerings (1 Samuel 10:8 AMP). It was about following the Lord's specific instructions, and honoring His commands. But after waiting the seven days, Saul decided he could no longer wait for Samuel to arrive. Samuel showed up later only to find Saul had already made the offering even though He was forbidden to do so (1 Samuel 13:11 AMP). Saul began explaining to Samuel his reasons as to what led him to make the offerings without Samuel, saying, "Since I saw that the people were scattering away from me.....I forced myself to offer the burnt offering" (1 Samuel 13:11-12 AMP). Saul was focused on the men who were with him, and saw that his help was fleeing from him, trembling in fear. I started to see how the influence from others had deterred him off of the pathway God had set for him. How his outward circumstances started to influence his inward convictions.

As I meditated on this part of the story deeply, I just could not get away from the words, "Let them scatter." The Lord began to speak to me, adding my name into the pages of Scripture: "Leslie, let them scatter." God has a way of speaking things to you, bringing to life the pages of Scripture, and applying it to the very situation you find yourself in. Tears started streaming down my face as I knew he was making this very personal to me in the area of struggling relationships. My husband and I have had many experiences of people "scattering" in our life, and it has been one of the most difficult things we've been through and it never seems to get easier each time we go through it. Relationships require you to be vulnerable, and more often than not in my own life, it has been worth every risk. But there have still been times where I have been left wondering, what did I do wrong? How could I have saved that friendship? If you are hurting today because of people who have left your life, whether by God's doing or reasons you don't even understand, know that you are not alone and that you are so loved by God.

Throughout my experiences in relationships,

God has taught me that I cannot allow relationships to define my relationship with Him. First and foremost. God has created us for community, and we need each other. But we can't let people have God's rightful place in our hearts. If you are focused on people and their presence in your life, you'll never be able to be used by God for the saving of many. If we are constantly focused on "who is with me" for validation on the completion of God's call on our lives, then we will never fulfill God's perfect and established plan. Your destiny is not dependent on them standing with you. Let them scatter. The truth is that people can only validate you based on their standards and experiences. People didn't give you the beautiful and unique calling on your life; God did. He is the faithful one to finish the work that He has started in you (Philippians 1:6 AMP). If there are people surrounding you that are hindering you from being obedient to what God is telling you, then it's okay to let them walk away. It may only be for a season, and God has a purpose and a plan for them too.

Don't misunderstand me. It's wonderful and biblical to have godly men and women surround you and encourage you (I thank God for the people He has gifted us with!), but if you are looking to them for your victory, you will be sorely disappointed. Saul had looked around and saw his people leaving him just before battle. Right in the middle of his greatest time of need, his people were abandoning him. Have you been there before? Instead of staying obedient to God, he became afraid and did what he thought would satisfy his relationships and lead him to victory. Don't do something forbidden (so to speak) to keep friends. Don't compromise your relationship with God based on what others are doing. Don't see your hope in people; see your hope in God. Don't see your solutions in people; see your solutions in God. If we center our lives around what we feel a person wants us to do, and we have to "force" ourselves to be something we aren't just to keep a relationship, we'll never hear and be obedient to what God is calling us to do, and in the end, we'll lose ourselves.

ONE MORE THING

Now I am speaking to you as to what God is about to do in your life as you trust His way and wait on Him. God is about to give you a strategy. When Samuel directed Saul to wait on him before making the sacrifice before going into battle, he said, "[W]ait seven days until I come to you and show you what you must do" (1 Samuel 10:8 AMP). In 1 Samuel 13:13, Samuel said this to Saul after his act of disobedience: "You have acted foolishly.....for [if you had obeyed] the Lord would have established your kingdom over Israel forever" (AMP). Our obedience unlocks the blessings of the Lord. When we honor Him and His word, He will use us to do mighty things for the kingdom of God. God wants to give you battle plans in your place of prayer that you won't get unless you wait on Him. God is about to give you what is needed to see deliverance in your finances, your mind, your physical health, your family! You don't want to miss His instructions. Let them scatter.

DAY 14:
DON'T STOP THERE

David said, "The Lord who rescued me from the paw of the lion and from the paw of the bear, He will rescue me from the hand of this Philistine." And Saul said to David, "Go, and may the Lord be with you. 1 Samuel 17:37 AMP

At the beginning of each year my husband and I open up our prayer jar to reflect on all the answered prayers from the previous year. We read things like the promise of our third baby boy fulfilled, home repairs taken care of, friendships restored, friends sharing the news of pregnancy after experiencing loss, the internet working correctly so that my husband could work efficiently, daily provision after leaving my job to be home with my kids, and on and on. It encouraged us so much to think on how God had moved in our lives, and in the lives of those we love.

But, as we emptied our jar to prepare for this year, I heard three words: "Don't Stop There." The Lord encouraged and challenged us to be bold in our prayers, to believe Him for more this next year than ever before. To posture my heart to seek Him first in all things (Matthew 6:33 AMP).

One of the references He spoke to me about was David. A young shepherd boy who took out the giant everyone was afraid of (1 Samuel 17 PARA). He highlighted to me the stones that David picked up to hit the giant on the head, knocking him off his feet (vv. 48-50 PARA). Can you imagine seeing this big, strong, warrior knocked to his feet by something so small? These stones represented David's history with God. How God delivered him from previous battles with lesser opponents than this giant, but David believed the result would be the same. Victory!

Every answered prayer is a stone. A stone that speaks that my God can do all things. A stone that represents God's love, power, and faithfulness. This stone of remembrance was to be my weapon for when doubt and discouragement try to speak the loudest. I started seeing this play out in my own life. I homeschool our oldest son, and we often will start the day with something he enjoys doing to give him encouragement to push through the hard things. I believe this is what God is saying. Look back, reflect, and be encouraged in the times God has been there, and know He will be again. Start this day, this month, this year with remembrance, and take your next step with confidence that God is with you and for you.

ONE MORE THING

I would encourage you to make your own prayer jar if you don't already have one. Place it where you can see it easily with some scrap paper and a pen beside it, ready to write. This will make it easier for you to remember to keep writing. You'll be amazed by all God's blessings throughout the year that we can so easily forget. We also write prayer requests and promises we are believing in God for. When a prayer is answered we write the date on the paper to help us remember when it took place. I promise, you will be so blessed in doing this that you'll do it year after year!

DAY 15:
THERE WILL BE AN "AFTER"

Then the virgin will rejoice in the dance, and the young men and old, together, For I will turn their mourning into joy and will comfort them and make them rejoice after their sorrow. I will fully satisfy the soul of the priests with abundance, and My people will be satisfied with My goodness," says the Lord. Jeremiah 31:13-14 AMP

Troubles can seem so overwhelming at times, leaving you wondering: How much more, Lord? But the Lord promises that because of His loving-kindness we will not be consumed (Lamentations 3:22 AMP). That He will come to our rescue, and no matter the size of the storm, we will be unharmed! Our circumstances seem so small in the light of His promises.

My husband and I were put between a rock and a hard place. We could see a person that we love headed down a dark path, and our concern began to consume us. It was difficult to watch, and even more difficult because this person didn't want help. As we were concerned for this beloved individual, we also knew that we needed to have boundaries in place to protect our family. I remember one night, in the heat of this situation, I went to lay down to try and rest. I remember tossing and turning with worry and fear that the battle would never end. I couldn't see a solution outside of this person changing their habits and getting the help they desperately needed. In my weariness, I turned my thoughts to the Lord. I started to think about what God could do in the midst of this situation. I was led to Jeremiah 31, where I was reminded of the Lord's comfort and the words "after their sorrow" leapt off the page! It was like a switch went off, and I felt an assurance that I may be in a battle today, but it will not last forever! Parts of that situation did finally come to a good end. We finally experienced relief from the turbulence and started to fervently intercede in prayer for this individual. Although we are still praying and believing for this prodigal to come home, we are trusting that God is working a miracle, and He has continued to guide and direct our path in the midst of it.

You may find yourself in the heat of a battle today. Did the word "after" cause you to release some much needed tears of joy? Or make you want to shout with expectation? My friend, there will be an after the battle. Although it may seem like it has taken much time already, it will not go on forever. May the Lord's comfort keep you in the storm as He has for me many times. May you know how loved you are, and that nothing escapes His attention. Your situation does not scare Him away. Romans 8: 38-39 tells us that nothing can separate us from His love. Love is a strong force against the darkness. Like me, you are standing in the perfect spot to witness a miracle! To see the hand of God move miraculously in your situation and cause you to know and trust His faithfulness more and more.

> *I am attacked from all sides, but you will rescue me unharmed by the battle.* Psalm 55:18 CEV

ONE MORE THING

I want to leave you with a scripture that I would speak during this time, almost every night. It was the only way I could sleep and rest in the midst of all the uncertainty. It was from Psalm 4:8: "I will both lie down and sleep in peace, for You alone, Lord, make me live in safety" (HCSB). I have memorized this scripture now, and it has become a nightly prayer over my children. We may not want to be in the battle, but those are the times I've experienced the hand of God most at work in my own heart and in my life. Those are the times I've clung to His Word like my life depended on it, and it came to my rescue every single time. The Scriptures become healing in the deep places of our heart, and we then begin to live from the very Words of God. I am believing for an "after their sorrow" moment for you. I am believing God for your breakthrough. Even though you may feel attacked on all sides today, as the Psalm speaks of, I declare over you that where there has been an attack on every side, there will now be PEACE on every side!

> *So he said to Judah, "Let us build these cities and surround them with walls, towers, gates and bars [to secure the doors]. The land is still ours because we have sought the LORD our*

God; we have sought Him [longing for Him with all our heart] and He has given us peace on every side." So they built and prospered. 2 Chronicles 14:7 AMP

DAY 16:
HEART CHECK

So are the paths of all who forget God; And the hope of the godless will perish, For his confidence is fragile and breaks, And his trust is [like] a spider's web. He trusts in his house, but it does not stand; He holds tightly to it, but it does not endure. Job 8:13-15 AMP

My husband and I bought an older renovated home that hadn't been lived in for nearly a year, so as you can imagine, we've encountered a few critters since we've moved in! I've gotten used to my boys fearlessly bringing me their critter friends all the time, but when they are in your house it's a whole different ball game! For a couple of weeks we would see spiders and their meticulous webs everywhere, and it was so interesting to me that as hard as those little spiders worked on those webs, they were so easily knocked down. Job 8:13-15 paints a clear picture of what happens when we place our trust and confidence in anything but God. The foundation eventually crumbles underneath us, leaving us feeling fragile and exposed.

Here are some red flags I've learned from along the way that I pray will keep you from creating your own spider webs! We are taught by the world to follow our hearts and it won't steer us wrong, but the Bible tells us the heart is deceitful above all things (Jeremiah 17:9 AMP). Trusting in our hearts causes us to focus too much attention on how we "feel" about something instead of what God's Word says. I am thankful for the times the Lord has protected me from what I thought I wanted for my life. The Bible also teaches us that influences matter, and when we put the weight of what others say over the weight of what God has said, we are in a dangerous place. Even placing our confidence in our roles and occupations, and then experiencing job loss and feeling like we've lost our security and purpose. Solomon said that he chased after the things that made his heart glad, yet he was still unfulfilled in them and it was as if chasing the wind (Ecclesiastes 2:10-11 AMP). Anything that we choose to lean on other than God is as stable as a spider's web. It breaks easily. Even the biggest spider's web can be taken down with ease.

But here's the good news! We can turn away from these other sources that do not profit us, but only take from us and cause more issues. We can humble our hearts before the Lord in full surrender, understanding our desperate need for Him and His ways because they truly are better! We then begin to experience a change from the inside out that becomes so bright to the world around us that even they say to us, "What is it about you that's different?" To which we answer with one name—Jesus—it's all because of Him! Even in the darkest of circumstances we THRIVE as children of God because our identity rests in Him. There is a promise of REST and BLESSED ASSURANCE in Christ that we are secure and protected by Him who holds all things together (Colossians 1:17 AMP)!

ONE MORE THING

My friend, renew your mind today and place your confidence in God and His word. Don't rely on yourself and your limited understanding. Hear the call of God to come up higher and receive a fresh perspective! Don't rely on that relationship to determine your value. Hear the call of God to go deeper in your relationship with Him! Start with these scriptures, and allow them to transform your mind and heart.

> *Be strong and courageous. Do not fear or be dismayed because of the king of Assyria, nor because of all the army that is with him; for the One with us is greater than the one with him. With him there is only an arm of flesh, but with us is the LORD our God to help us and to fight our battles." And the people relied on the words of Hezekiah king of Judah. 2 Chronicles 32:7-8 AMP*

> *Therefore let us [with privilege] approach the throne of grace [that is, the throne of God's gracious favor] with confidence and without fear, so that we may receive mercy [for our failures] and find [His amazing] grace to help in time of need [an appropriate blessing, coming just at the right moment]. Hebrews 4:16 AMP*

> *Whatever my eyes looked at with desire I did not refuse them. I did not withhold from my heart any pleasure, for my heart was pleased*

because of all my labor; and this was my reward for all my labor. Then I considered all which my hands had done and labored to do, and behold, all was vanity and chasing after the wind and there was no profit (nothing of lasting value) under the sun. Ecclesiastes 2:10-11 AMP

Blessed [with spiritual security] is the man who believes and trusts in and relies on the LORD And whose hope and confident expectation is the LORD. For he will be [nourished] like a tree planted by the waters, That spreads out its roots by the river; And will not fear the heat when it comes; But its leaves will be green and moist. And it will not be anxious and concerned in a year of drought Nor stop bearing fruit. The heart is deceitful above all things And it is extremely sick; Who can understand it fully and know its secret motives? I, the LORD, search and examine the mind, I test the heart, To give to each man according to his ways, According to the results of his deeds. Jeremiah 17:7-10 AMP

DAY 17:
TRUST ME IN THE FOG

Then He said to Thomas, Reach here with your finger, and see My hands; and put out your hand and place it in My side. Do not be unbelieving, but [stop doubting and] believe.
John 20:27 AMP

You know what can be the hardest thing sometimes.....being honest about the moments we struggle in our faith. We feel such shame about who we know we should be, that we forget that it was at the very point of humility and brokenness that we received salvation. If we focus too much on the times we aren't getting it all just right, we forget that it was from a place of struggling in our own messes that we realized our need for a Savior. I began to wonder, what else could be realized in these moments of doubt? Let's break the cycle, and instead of struggling through a place of shame and guilt, learn a better way to address our moments of doubt through the eyes of Jesus.

One evening on vacation, I was overlooking some beautiful mountain views, when suddenly a blanket of fog fell from the skies, and we couldn't see anything anymore. It was so thick and it spread quickly. But as we waited for a while, the fog dissipated and we could see all the breathtaking mountain ranges again even clearer than before! It was then that I heard the still small voice of the Lord whisper, "Trust me in the fog." He began to talk with me about being honest with Him about what I was feeling and my struggle to trust and believe.

In John 20:24-29, we see one of Jesus' disciples, Thomas, hearing all about his friends who had just seen Jesus appear to them after His resurrection. But Thomas wasn't easily convinced. He was likely still struggling with the swirling thoughts in his mind about Jesus, the promised Messiah, dying so brutally on the cross and wondering what would happen next. The "in-between" place where your faith is tested and unbelief is lurking. Thomas did something that can often be difficult to do. He was honest about where he was in his heart. He was honest about his struggle to believe, saying, "Unless I see in His hands the marks of the nails, and put my finger into the nail prints, and put my hand into His side, I will never believe" (v. 25 AMP). It was at that moment I knew that just like Thomas, I was too focused on what I couldn't see that I struggled to stand tall in my faith and trust in God's promises. But Jesus' response to this real moment in Thomas' life has changed everything for me.

The Bible says that eight days later, post Thomas' outward confession, the disciples were inside the house and Jesus Himself came through the doors that had been barred and stood among them, saying, "Peace to you" (v. 26 AMP). Then Jesus looked directly at Thomas and said, "Reach here with your finger, and see My hands; and put out your hand and place it in My side. Do not be unbelieving but [stop doubting and] believe" (v. 27 AMP). Thomas got to see Jesus in a new way in the honesty of his struggle. Even more amazing is that in all the times Jesus chose to reveal Himself post-resurrection, this was one of them! A Shepherd's response to His sheep, who had been struggling with doubt.

My eyes began to open to other times in the Bible where Jesus responded to doubt. In Matthew

14:28-31, Peter had made a bold request that Jesus would command him to come to Jesus on the water. Peter stepped out in faith and started walking on the water toward Jesus, but when he began to see the effects of the wind, he became frightened and started to sink into the water. He was standing directly in front of Jesus Himself and still struggled with doubt! In that moment he cried out to Jesus, "Lord, save me!" Immediately, Jesus extended His hand and caught him, saying, "O you of little faith, why did you doubt?" (vv. 30-31 AMP). Peter learned that day that Jesus' heart was not to condemn him for his struggle to believe, but to enhance his dependance on Jesus as the One who can reach down and pull him up out of any situation. Peter got to see Jesus in a new way in the honesty of his struggle.

{According to *The New Strong's Concordance*, the Greek word for doubt used in this passage is *distazo,* which means to waver in opinion (Strong 1996, 326).}

Could it be that Jesus wants to reveal Himself to you in a whole new way right here in your place of doubt? Even in my own life I can see that it was in the moments of feeling utterly defeated that He came to my rescue and I saw His eyes of love for me. Even in the struggles of Thomas and Peter, Jesus still chose them to be His very own. Instead of despising the struggle and feeling shame, go before the Lord and be honest with Him about it all. Let Him meet you where you are as you experience Him in a miraculous way.

PRAYER FOR TODAY

Lord Jesus, come through the door of our hearts and our homes! Break down any barrier keeping us from seeking and seeing You. We welcome You here! Meet us right here where we are in this place of struggle, confusion, and fear. I believe that what we release in these moments of honesty is Jeremiah 33:3, that we can call to You and You will answer, and You will tell us and show us great and mighty things that have been confined and hidden (PARA). Make Yourself known in this place. It's our heart's cry to know You more. Your presence changes everything. You drive out the darkness with Your light and love. Remind us that You are with us in the fog when we can't see the way forward. That You are extending Your hand to us in our places of doubt and pulling us up to be in the safety of Your arms. Draw us closer in. We want to know you more and more. In Your Name I Pray, Amen.

DAY 18:
HEAVEN'S ANGELS

For He will command His angels in regard to you, To protect and defend and guard you in all your ways [of obedience and service].
Psalm 91:11 AMP

When my firstborn was not quite two years old, he had to have surgery to remove his tonsils and adenoids. I still remember that feeling on the way to the hospital—absolute dread. My mind was thinking so many thoughts; he is too little to be having surgery, what if something goes wrong, what if he doesn't wake up from the anesthesia? You see my husband's family has a history of having severe negative responses to certain types of anesthesia. My husband and I prayed and prayed for our little boy that morning on the way to the hospital at 5 a.m. We prayed that God would be with him and his doctors, and that the procedure would be perfect. We also had a community of praying men and women covering him as well.

Fast forward to the moments before he went into the operating room. We had been taken to a new waiting room while the doctors came in to discuss the surgery, and then his nurses came to give him some medication to help him stay calm. All of a sudden it hit me as they were talking that I couldn't go back with him. No one could. Not me. Not my husband. Just him and the medical team. I was trying my best to hold back the tears for my little boy who didn't know what was about to happen. I looked up at the ceiling and I remember saying something like this: "Papa, I'm scared. I don't want to leave my little boy, he'll be all alone back there. He's just too little!" I dried my eyes quickly because I could see the nurses coming to take him back to the operating room. The nurses rolled the bed out of my reach heading towards those big double doors, and SUDDENLY my spiritual eyes were opened, and two angels appeared standing at the head of my son's bed wearing what looked like gladiator armor from head to toe! One angel looked toward me and nodded. I remember his eyes were crystal blue, and then he turned around as they both walked back through the big double doors to the operating room with my boy. It was nothing short of miraculous! My eyes filled with tears, my heart full of joy, and my emotions calm with supernatural peace as I went out to the waiting room because I knew that my son was not alone. His Heavenly Father had His eyes on him and He had charged His angels to guard and protect my son.

> *See to it that you don't despise one of these little ones, because I tell you that in heaven their angels continually view the face of my Father in heaven.* Matthew 18:10 CSB

> *"Don't be afraid," the prophet answered. "Those who are with us are more than those who are with them." And Elisha prayed, "Open his eyes, Lord, so that he may see." Then the Lord opened the servant's eyes, and he looked and saw the hills full of horses and chariots of fire all around Elisha. 2 Kings 6:16-17 NIV*

ONE MORE THING

After my son successfully came out of surgery, my husband and I talked about all that had happened that day. He shared with me a few words of encouragement that I would like to also share with you.

Greg-As parents, we want what's best for our kids, and to care for them and protect them. We have been through a handful of situations with our children over the last few years, and I can tell you that we have seen God work in small ways and then perform miracles in our situations. We ask Him to help us, and He always meets us where we are, and just like it says in Matthew 7, if we as earthly parents care that much for our children, how much more does He care for us? We just need to ask, and He is faithful to provide.

> *You parents—if your children ask for a loaf of bread, do you give them a stone instead? Or if they ask for a fish, do you give them a snake? Of course not! So if you sinful people know how to give good gifts to your children, how much more will your heavenly Father give good gifts to those who ask him.* Matthew 7:9-11 NLT

PRAYER FOR TODAY

Lord Jesus, open my eyes today that I may see that there are more for me than there are against me. I am not alone despite what my thoughts are shouting. I give You my fears, and I hear Your whisper, saying, "Don't be afraid." You are in the places I can't even reach. When we drop our son off at preschool, I know You are with him. To my family members too far for my reach, I know You are with them too. I know You are keeping watch over my life, and the lives of those I love as I give them back to You. In confident trust I pray, Amen. (Scripture reference: 2 Kings 6:16 NIV)

DAY 19:
WHAT IS YOUR HIM?

David said to Saul, "Let no man's courage fail because of <u>him</u> (Goliath)...." 1 Samuel 17:32 AMP

As we go back into 1 Samuel 17 to just before David comes on the scene, we see Saul and his men frightened by a Philistine champion who had great height and strength (vv. 4-7). Their courage had faltered at the sight of this giant. Is there a "him" in your life too? It may look like financial problems, troubled family relationships, physical health issues, or hurtful words spoken against you causing discouragement. If it isn't coming clear to you as to what your "him" might be, ask God to search your heart and reveal to you if there is a "him" in your life that is shaking your courage. Then take a look at David and Saul's conversation about what to do about this "him."

Then Saul said to David, "You are not able to go against this Philistine to fight him. For you are [only] a young man and he has been a warrior since his youth." But David said to Saul, "Your servant was tending his father's sheep. When a lion or a bear came and took a lamb out of the flock, I went out after it and attacked it and rescued the lamb from its mouth; and when it rose up against me, I seized it by its whiskers and struck and killed it. Your servant has killed both the lion and the bear; and this uncircumcised Philistine will be like one of them, SINCE he has taunted and defied the armies of the living God." David said, "The LORD who rescued me from the paw of the lion and from the paw of the bear, He will rescue me from the hand of this Philistine." (1 Samuel 17:33-37a AMP, emphasis added)

One way you can know if your courage has been shaken is the way you speak about your problem. David didn't speak in agreement with Saul, nor did he look at himself and feel limited by his outward appearance and skill. He just simply spoke of God's faithfulness. He shared his testimony of the victories given to him by God. David was saying the situation may look different, but my God is the same. He delivered me from the battles in my past and will rescue me from the hand of this Philistine. My God's strength and ability is not limited by the size of what's coming against me!

What if we changed our focus from our problem to the faithfulness of our God? The Bible says that Goliath came out morning and evening, and took his stand for 40 DAYS, taunting the Israelites to send someone out there to fight him (vv. 8-25). I can tell you I have looked at my problem with the same perspective as Saul more times than I'd like to admit. Allowing that problem to taunt me and stare me in the face day after day. Maybe you're like me and have been quick to align with fear instead of standing in faith. I want to encourage you as I often encourage myself to declare the goodness of your God by recounting all the times He's come through for you and others you love. David said let no man's courage fail because of *him*! Goliath's defeat was sealed the day he decided to stand up against God's chosen ones, and so it will be for your giant!

ONE MORE THING

Check your intake. It may be helpful to determine if what you are taking in is causing you to stumble. The Bible says in Matthew 6:22, "The eye is the lamp of the body; so if your eye is clear [spiritually perceptive], your whole body will be full of light [benefiting from God's precepts]" (AMP). I have found that outside sources sometimes cause me to focus more on my problem, and my own limitations, than on what God can do. Boundaries may need to be in place to minimize distractions. Ask God to reveal to you if there is anything in your life that is causing you more harm than good. We can step out of fear today, and start walking in faith.

DAY 20:
COMFORT ZONES

Do not remember the former things, Or ponder the things of the past. Listen carefully, I am about to do a new thing, Now it will spring forth; Will you not be aware of it? I will even put a road in the wilderness, Rivers in the desert. Isaiah 43:18-19 AMP

Can you really set aside the past and press on to the new thing God has for you? I remember traveling with my family and asking God this same question. We were on the way to visit extended family, and typically don't need the GPS because we know the way as we've traveled it many times before. But this particular day we decided to use the GPS just to see exactly what time we'd be there. It told us to take an exit we were not familiar with so we ignored it and went on the way we were most familiar with. We later ended up in traffic taking us much longer to get to our family than planned. My husband and I looked at each other and knew that if we'd followed the change in direction, creating a new way to lead us away from the traffic, we would have been nearly there! But there we were, stuck in traffic.

This made me think about what it means to open your heart and mind to when God is leading you in a new direction. Truth is, we can't always see what's ahead of us in life! Sometimes when we only go the way we know, we miss new opportunities that God has created for us. I'm all for adventure, but I also like to be comfortable. I started to think more about that word, comfortable. If we stay in our comfort zone, then we rely on our own strength to accomplish the task. We become the "able" one in our comfortable place. The Holy Spirit is named our Comforter in the Bible (John 14:26 AMP). When we step out of our comfort zone, we can rely on the Lord's comfort, and He becomes our "able."

God is searching the earth looking for those who will go "off roadin" with Him. To lay down the plans we've made and trust in the plans that God has for us, which were established before the beginning of time. We often want to see the new thing, but are we willing to create it with Him? Following Him even when we aren't sure where we are headed.

As hard as it is, we aren't supposed to know everything! His thoughts and ways are higher than ours, so we can trust that He can see beyond what we see with our eyes enough to orchestrate the perfect plan. This was such a good reminder for me that He's got a plan, it's a good one, and as I follow Him and do things His way, I will surely see the goodness of the Lord in my life! But you know what else? Even when we have those moments where we rely on our own understanding and take the familiar path, He always graciously leads us back to the path He designed and says, Come with me, I want to show you a new thing, better than anything you could ask or imagine! (Ephesians 3:20 PARA).

PRAYER FOR TODAY

Lord Jesus, help me today to step out onto the water with You. I may not know the details of where we are headed, but I do know You. I place my trust in You, and know that You are faithful. In Your Name I pray, Amen. (Scripture reference: Matthew 14:28-29)

DAY 21:
GIVE STRIFE THE BOOT!

If possible, as far as it depends on you, live at peace with everyone. Romans 12:18 AMP

What is strife?[7] *Merriam-Webster Dictionary* describes it as an act of contention. A fight. A struggle. You can literally feel strife in a room. It's that potent. The Bible tells us that we can make a difference in driving out strife from our lives. I love today's verse from Romans because it shows us that we play a part in creating peace instead of strife. This can be no easy task. I want to give you an example from my own life that taught me how to deal with strife.

I have been blessed with a wonderful husband, who loves the Lord with all his heart, and is devoted to our family. But, of course, we have disagreements just like everyone else! We are two different people, with our own thoughts and desires, learning how to love each other better everyday. I remember one particular day when we were so aggravated with each other over a pile of little things, that my gentle spirited husband said to me, "I'll watch the kids, you go and enjoy some me-time today!" Although it was a kind gesture, I was not amused by his offer. It felt like he was saying it was me that was the problem!

It seemed like every time we tried to reconcile our disagreement, we would end up arguing about our differing points of view of the situation. We knew we needed help! So we made ourselves sit down together with our kids as we explained to them that we still love each other even though we were having a lot of "discussions," and made sure to mention that handling your frustrations with anger was not what was right. It's okay to let your kids know you're not perfect at times! Then, we all four sat together and prayed. I will be honest in saying I didn't feel like praying at that moment. I just began to sob quietly with my head down because I was too prideful to let my husband hear it, and whispered the confessions of my heart about all the things I had said that I wished I hadn't. I was having a silent conversation back and forth with the Lord in my head, to which His reply was reminding me I needed to forgive just as He forgave and continues to forgive me, and that He would restore the intimacy in my marriage again as He always restores my soul when I come to Him about anything. And the word MERCY was resounding in my head. I knew as soon as I opened my eyes and looked up at my husband, something was going to be different about us from that moment forward.

I looked up and the burden of once felt aggravation and heaviness was lifted! I mean gone! All I felt was pure joy! I didn't feel angry or frustrated anymore about all the little things. I just saw my husband, and I was thankful for him. We reconciled, and our time together and as a family, was that much sweeter than before. I learned through this moment that the way to handle strife is to pray. Prayer releases God's power to intercept that situation. If I hadn't prayed in this moment, I would've given the enemy an open door to wreak havoc. We then can make a decision to keep peace in the relationship if it's in our power to do so. I'm not saying that this is always possible. But you can step out of strife within your own heart by praying and giving it over to the Lord. He can heal your pain and disappointment, and in His overwhelming mercy, help you to forgive and release healing in the situation. This will not always be something you will feel like doing. But God would not tell us to forgive if it wasn't even possible.

ONE MORE THING

Start with a simple prayer, and let the Spirit of God begin to pray through you. There are many times I will start to pray, and words will begin to flow out that I wasn't even thinking about. One of my favorite scriptures is Colossians 1:17, which says, "And He Himself existed and is before all things, and in Him all things hold together" (AMP). Isn't it so encouraging to know that He holds it all together! Just when you feel everything is falling apart you can rest in the truth that He is present and in control. When we pray we are inviting God to come into our out of control situation, and possibilities begin to arise like never before.

PRAYER FOR TODAY

Lord Jesus, I lay this situation weighing heavily on my heart at Your feet. I surrender my desire to control, and I ask Your forgiveness for trying to take the reins, thinking that I know better than You. I lay my desires down for Yours. Change my heart to match Yours. In Your Name I pray, Amen.

DAY 22:
REJECTION STINGS

You are always and dearly loved by God! So robe yourself with virtues of God, since you have been divinely chosen to be holy. Be merciful as you endeavor to understand others, and be compassionate, showing kindness toward all. Be gentle and humble, unoffendable in your patience with others.
Colossians 3:12 TPT

Belonging is a part of who we are, and when we are not accepted by a person or particular group of people, it's hard. I made a list for myself of my own reactions to rejection. One being every time you get on social media you leave feeling empty and that something is missing in your life. Two is that you start to reject people to protect yourself before you are rejected by them first. Three is that you begin to overthink everything you say and do. Four, you begin to do and say the things you think people want you to say and do because you crave their validation and approval. All very true. I made this list after I started reflecting on the ways I have responded to rejection throughout the years. It stings. I curl up in a ball on the inside and want to hide away from it all, never to experience pain again.

Like I have said before, God is not afraid of your emotions. He doesn't sit back, rolling His eyes, saying you're ridiculous for feeling that way. No, He listens. He sits with you, and reminds you that He too knows that feeling of rejection. I started to unpack my thoughts on the rejection I was so painfully experiencing and found commonality with several people in the Bible.

In the Garden of Eden, Eve was tempted by the devil with one lie that said you don't have everything you need. From that moment on they were awakened to their weaknesses, naked and afraid, and aware of all the dangers all around them. It shook them and impacted every generation after them. But I noticed the Father came to them in the garden speaking and demonstrating hope. Although they had aligned themselves with a lie spoken so cleverly, the Father came in with clothes. He came in with provision and reminded them He is still all they need. Although things would be different, He had not abandoned them (Genesis 3 PARA).

I remember Mary who carried the promised Messiah. As the child grew every day, she kept quiet, knowing that there would be others who would not understand her. Mary could only share in this blessed time with Elizabeth, the mother of John the Baptist. Mary had one friend to share with in the most crucial time of her life. It seems having many voices around you is not always what's best. Why should we then count the number of those who are with us, and instead look around and take notice of the fruitful relationships that God has blessed us with. Be thankful for the one or two relationships that are working instead of giving all our attention to the ones that are not. We could be at risk of damaging the ones that are fruitful for lack of attention (Luke 1 PARA).

Have you ever thought about when Peter met Jesus? Jesus approached two boats, but He walked up to the boat belonging to Peter. Jesus used his boat to preach the gospel to the crowd. He picked Peter even when there were other options. This tells me that Jesus intentionally chose me and you. He chose us to call His own. He claims us even when others have rejected us and our weaknesses (Luke 5 PARA).

I was challenged in the story of Saul to cling to what God has spoken about me and not what others are saying or not saying. Saul had an anointing on his life to be King, yet when he saw his men rejecting him, he responded by doing what was pleasing to them. As hard as it is to admit it, I've been in this position too. I had to make a decision about whether I would trust God or trust the people around me (1 Samuel 13 PARA).

After a time of true reflection, prayer, and fasting, I realized that I had been holding back parts of myself and my giftings because of rejection. I remember writing in my journal this statement while in prayer: "You're not just an introverted person, you are afraid of rejection. You're holding back." I had held to the excuse that I was just shy and introverted, but really I was only kidding myself. The more I tried to hold back, the worse I felt inside. I couldn't stay in this place. I had a decision to make.

Jesus has proven to be a better friend than any one person could be for me on this earth. And it's also true that relationships are important and that we should keep peace with everyone as long as it is in our power to do so. But we must stay true to ourselves amidst the disapproval of other people. We will answer for our own actions and not for others. We can't use blame as a scapegoat for not being obedient to God. I was afraid of rejection because I had believed the same lie that Eve had believed. That I'm missing something. But the truth is, I already have everything I need. I have something to offer, and you have something to offer too. I had given people places in my heart that didn't belong to them, and when they were gone I was left empty. I put myself in a dangerous position. I remember one day the Lord speaking to me as I was looking outside my dining room window. I felt the Lord saying that He wanted to heal me completely from the wounds of rejection, but I had to look away from the window (so to speak). He was saying I had to stop looking at what other people are doing and set my gaze on Him. To hear His voice above the noise, and stay anchored in His word.

You are significant, loved, and chosen. It's not having the most relationships, having the most likes on social media, or even accomplishing all your goals. It's looking into the eyes of the One who made you, formed you in your mother's womb, and has every right to speak over you. We get to display the virtues and perfections of Him who called us out of darkness and into His marvelous light (1 Peter 2:9 AMP). His thoughts toward you are precious, His love toward you is unending, and He is always there to lift your head (Psalm 139 PARA).

With the revelation of who I am in Christ reshaping my heart, I began to make some changes with help from the Holy Spirit. I set boundaries for myself on social media. I started smiling a lot more, and having conversations with people in public without fear. I want people to know that Jesus loves them. I want to get out of the way and reflect His light for the world to see within me. I want to give Him all the glory for what He has done in my life and declare His goodness from the highest mountain to the lowest valley. I want to be slow to anger, quick to forgive, and beware of the negative assumptions my mind likes to create (James 1:19 AMP).

PRAYER FOR TODAY

Lord Jesus, forgive me for the ways I have looked to others for what only You can give me. For giving up Your rightful place in my heart in fear of man. I repent for the idols I have made out of relationships. Heal the sting of rejection in my heart, and help me to love and unselfishly seek the best for others. Your love enables me to love others as it grows out of Your love for me. It was You who first loved me. It was You who chose me first. The more I grow to understand Your unconditional love for me, the greater capacity I have to love others. I can love difficult people and turn away from offense when I come daily into Your sanctuary and embrace Your love for me. It has the power to heal and restore and transform our desires to match Yours. Let Your light shine from within me in such a way that others see my good deeds and glorify You! In Jesus' Name, Amen. (Scripture references: 1 John 4:7; John 15:16; Matthew 5:16)

I don't want to be quick to end this day without giving you scriptures to meditate on in this area of rejection. I would encourage you to make it a part of your daily routine to read, pray, and speak aloud these scriptures. Let them transform your mind and cause you to feel hope again in the area of relationships. We are ONE body, and we need YOU!

Romans 12:5 AMP: "...so we, who are many, are [nevertheless just] one body in Christ, and individually [we are] parts one of another [mutually dependent on each other]."

1 Peter 3:15-16 AMP: "But in your hearts set Christ apart [as holy—acknowledging Him, giving Him first place in your lives] as Lord.

Always be ready to give a [logical] defense to anyone who asks you to account for the hope and confident assurance [elicited by faith] that is within you, yet [do it] with gentleness and respect. And see to it that your conscience is entirely clear, so that every time you are slandered or falsely accused, those who attack or disparage your good behavior in Christ will be shamed [by their own words]."

2 Timothy 1:12 AMP: "This is why I suffer as I do. Still, I am not ashamed; for I know Him [and I am personally acquainted with Him] whom I have believed [with absolute trust and confidence in Him and in the truth of His deity], and I am persuaded [beyond any doubt] that He is able to guard that which I have entrusted to Him until that day [when I stand before Him]."

Matthew 5:16 AMP: "Let your light shine before men in such a way that they may see your good deeds and moral excellence, and [recognize and honor and] glorify your Father who is in heaven."

Revelation 22:12 AMP: "Behold, I (Jesus) am

coming quickly, and My reward is with Me, to give to each one according to the merit of his deeds (earthly works, faithfulness)."

Romans 12:20 TPT: "If your enemy is hungry, buy him lunch! Win him over with kindness. For your surprising generosity will awaken his conscience, and God will reward you with favor."

1 Thessalonians 5:15 NIV: "Make sure that nobody pays back wrong for wrong, but always strive to do what is good for each other and for everyone else."

DAY 23:
MAKE THE INVESTMENT

So He continued preaching in the synagogues of Judea [the country of the Jews, including Galilee]. Luke 4:44 AMP

My dear friend, I am praying for you. I feel the pain and anguish of your heart as I write these words to you. I know your heart has been wounded. I know it feels like the pain will never end, and your situation will never get better. But I'm a living testimony that it is going to get better. It can feel like you are such a blessing to some people, seeing how God is using you to minister to them, and to others it seems they would rather not associate with you. How can this be?

I hope by giving you an inside glimpse at my own life experiences, you will begin to see and understand that we truly understand very little when it comes to the full picture. And we need the Holy Spirit to impart wisdom to us and give us understanding beyond what we see. I remember one Christmas season I was feeling so rejected by a beloved friend. I didn't know what I had done or what I had said. But I knew this friend was pushing me away. I remember it because it was especially hard around Christmas time. It's a season that we are more intentional to express our love in action through gift giving and acts of service. I was feeling so distraught one day that I think I had cried the whole day. I loved this friend, and it was so very hurtful that they were avoiding me altogether. What was worse was that they didn't feel they could be honest with me about what they were feeling, in hopes that we could reconcile.

One day I got a text from another friend asking if she could come over for a visit. She had something she wanted to give me. I thought this was just what I needed, a friend! This friend had no idea what I was going through. Thank you Lord for sending this friend to uplift me, I prayed! My friend came and she shared with me how much of a blessing my husband and I had been to her family. She expressed so much love and gratitude with her kind words, that I almost had trouble receiving it. I was still seeing through the lens of rejection. Then she handed me a gift and left to be with her family. As she left I remember looking up and saying, Lord, how can I be a blessing to some and not to others? It was an honest question in my confusion. Rejection was trying its best to tell me that I was not any of the things that my dear friend had spoken about. His response to me were the words, "So it was with me." He took me to Luke 4:44.

In Luke 4 Jesus came to His hometown Nazareth, and because it was the Sabbath, He went to the synagogue (vv. 16-21). He stood up to read from Isaiah and as He finished, with everyone listening attentively, He told them He was the Messiah that was foretold of in these scriptures. It appeared that at first they marveled at His words, but their hearts began to turn against Him in disbelief. They could not believe that someone they knew so well was the one the Scriptures of old were talking about (v. 22). They did not receive Jesus or His words (vv. 23-28). In their anger and rage they made plans to push him off a cliff (v. 29)! This is some very deep rejection by His friends, His family, and His community! Jesus truly understands what we are feeling. Then I read further down to verse 31 where Jesus had left His hometown and went to another town in Galilee. There He continued to teach, and the people were amazed by His words! While there He drove out demons, and every sick person that was brought to Him was cured (vv. 33-41). It was a very different reaction than He found in His hometown. The people of Capernaum were so amazed by the miracles happening there, they came looking for Him and tried to prevent Him from leaving them! But He told them that He must preach the good news to other cities and towns (vv. 42-44). The words "So He continued preaching" in Luke 4:44 grabbed me as I was reading this chapter. The Lord began to show me that not everyone will be for you, and rejection may even come from those closest to you. But don't let it stop you! Keep being who God has called you to be. Keep loving others and investing in relationships! God has entrusted you with something special. Jesus experienced both rejection and approval, and He wasn't deterred or motivated by either. The enemy wants us focused on the hurt so that we give up on relationships, but God is enabling us to love radically. God puts in us a heart of compassion in exchange for the rejection. That's healing. You will love better today because of what you have been through! It is worth the risk to step out and be vulnerable. What would've happened if

Jesus stopped and didn't go to another town or city? Jesus didn't let it stop Him from doing what He was destined to do. He continued preaching.

A spiritual mother in my life once gave me words of wisdom on this very topic. She said, "Don't allow what *they* think to keep you out of what *God* thinks. He hasn't changed His mind about you. When you share your vulnerability, that's when and where you're anointed. Don't let assumptions lead you astray. Recenter yourself on the truth you know and He knows about your heart, and leave the assumptions and what you don't know to Him." She would often remind me of 1 Corinthians 15:58: "Be steadfast, immovable, always excelling in the work of the Lord [always doing your best and doing more than is needed], being continually aware that your labor [even to the point of exhaustion] in the Lord is not futile nor wasted [it is never without purpose]" (AMP). Let this scripture breathe life back into you today!

ONE MORE THING

During this season I would often see the numbers 444 all around me. I would look at the clock and see 4:44, or I would pay for something at a store, and the amount would be $4.44. Everytime I see those numbers I think of Luke 4:44, and I pray that God would enable me to keep moving forward and walk out His purpose for my life. That the Lord would keep me from the temptation to have validation and approval from others. That He would protect me as I take the risk of being vulnerable in relationships. That as I pour out to others what He has given me, He will pour back into me.

DAY 24:
YOU'VE BEEN BUILT INTO THE WALL

So she let them down by a rope through the window, for the house she lived in was part of the city wall. Joshua 2:15 NIV

What if I told you that you are in the perfect position right where you are to be used by God? You are in the position for a purpose. You've been built into the wall like Rahab. I remember jotting down these words in my journal as I was reading Joshua 2. I pondered to myself, "Am I in position, God, and didn't even know it?" You see, I had been so focused on where I wasn't. Goals that hadn't been accomplished. Doors had been shut. Feeling unfulfilled. I had been praying for God to show me what He wanted me to do. I truly wanted to stay faithful, even in the waiting, but my faith was growing weary.

Rahab had heard about the Israelites and how their God had rescued them and given them the land occupied by her people, saying to the two Israelite spies, "I know that the Lord has given you this land and that a great fear of you has fallen on us, so that all who live in this country are melting in fear because of you. We have heard how the Lord dried up the water of the Red Sea for you when you came out of Egypt, and what you did to Sihon and Og, the two kings of the Amorites east of the Jordan, whom you completely destroyed. When we heard of it, our hearts melted in fear and everyone's courage failed because of you, for the Lord your God is God in heaven above and on the earth below" (Joshua 2:9-11 NIV). She knew the spies were scouting out the city in preparation to take the land, so she made a bold request that the Israelites would show kindness to her family and save their lives (v.12-13). They agreed to her request with a few conditions, and "she let them down by a rope through the window, for the house she lived in was part of the city wall" (v. 15 NIV). I meditated on this verse, pondering Rahab's unique position in the placement of her home. It wasn't by accident that it was her home that served as a place of shelter and safety for the spies. Rahab didn't know that she was in the perfect position to be used by God for a great purpose. Because of her position in the wall around Jericho the spies were able to escape unseen, and they kept their promise to protect her and her family. This truth awakened my heart to the reality that we serve a God who is intentional! Nothing is wasted in Him. He uses it all. Rahab was not someone who was esteemed in her community, and I'm sure many thought less of her because she was a prostitute. But God chose her!

Friend, we are standing in position for God to use us for a far greater purpose than we have yet realized! He's been preparing us all the while! He has purposely placed us where we are today to fulfill a purpose that He has set in His heart. That He planned while we were yet in our mother's womb! I pray the truth that you too are in position for a purpose rests deeply into your heart, giving you such an expectation for what God is doing in your life! Don't believe the lie that your wrong doings are too great to ever be used by God. You don't have to have a special title, a perfect track record, or have highly esteemed connections to faithfully serve God.

Rahab believed in her heart that the Israelite God was the one true God, and we see her confessing her need for Him in the Scriptures. God redeemed her story, and she is part of the lineage of King David and Jesus (Matthew 1:5 AMP)! Once you confess with your mouth as Rahab did, that "the Lord your God is God," and believe in your heart, you are now a part of a new family, the family of God (Joshua 2:11 NIV)! The Bible says in Isaiah 49:16, "I have engraved you on the palms of my hands" (NIV). You belong to Him! He claims you as His own, and others will see His claim as He cares for your cause. The things that you are passionate for, the desires of your heart given to you by God.

PRAYER FOR TODAY

Lord Jesus, I thank You for awakening a greater purpose within me. I had counted myself out, but Your loving-kindness pulled me back in. You remind me that Your grace is sufficient for me, and that Your power finds its full expression through my weakness. You have revived hope within me today. I love You, Lord! In Your Name I pray, Amen. (Scripture reference: 2 Corinthians 12:9 TPT)

DAY 25:
STAND YOUR GROUND

Joshua said to the priests, "Take up the ark of the covenant and cross over [the river] ahead of the people." So they took up the ark of the covenant and went on ahead of the people.
Joshua 3:6 AMP

I know that both you and I have something in common. No matter what our backgrounds may be, we both have unsaved people in our lives. Whether it be a friend or a family member, we both can think of at least one person right now that we've been praying for to receive salvation. We may even find ourselves carrying this loved one to the feet of Jesus day after day, with no evidence on the outside that it is even making a difference.

At our first home my husband and I had a walk-in closet. I would go in there with my Bible every morning to hear from God. I had some very precious times with the Lord in that closet and many tear stained pages in my Bible. One day as I was praying for a loved one, I went into a vision. The Lord often shows me things through visions, perhaps because I am such a visual learner. In the vision I saw myself with my feet planted in the dirt, water standing tall to my right and to my left, and on my back I was carrying the Ark of the Covenant. It looked like I had stepped back in time to the exact moment the Levitical priests had stepped into the Jordan River and the waters parted miraculously. The waters would remain cut off, allowing the entire nation of Israel to cross over, while the priests stood firm holding the Ark of the Covenant (Joshua 3:17 PARA). As I looked up I saw multitudes of people passing by, crossing over to the other side. Then I saw this loved one. It was as if their face was shining brightly in the sun. I saw them walking with the crowd, crossing over the Jordan River too. I heard the Lord speak to me, saying, "You carry my Spirit inside of you, and as you stand firm in your faith in Me, your witness will lead them to Me.

Your prayers will open up their ears to hear Me." I was stunned by such words! Tears of joy streaming down my face. I've clung to hope for this person ever since, never giving up on praying for them! I have seen the evidence of this since that time, and witnessed how the Lord has been working in their life.

I share all of this to encourage you today to not give up! Don't give up on your loved ones. Don't stop praying. You're making a difference to those God has placed around you! God is using your life to shine His light and love through you for them to see and experience. Don't lose heart. As it says in Galatians 6:9, "Let us not become weary in doing good, for at the proper time we will reap a harvest if we do not give up" (NIV). Keep interceding for your loved ones. Keep standing in faith regardless of what you see in the natural. God has a plan for their lives, and it is by our prayers that we partner with God in His pursuit of their hearts. He loves them, even more than we do.

PRAYER FOR TODAY

Heavenly Father, I thank You for strengthening me by Your word. Your words to me change everything, and I cling to them as daily bread. Your comfort reminds me to rest in Your faithfulness. I entrust my loved ones to You, knowing that You are passionately pursuing them. Rescue them just as You rescued me. In Jesus' Name, Amen. (Scripture references: Matthew 6:11; 2 Timothy 1:12)

DAY 26:
HE'S STILL WITH YOU

Every single moment you are thinking of me! How precious and wonderful to consider that you cherish me constantly in your every thought! O God, your desires toward me are more than the grains of sand on every shore! When I awake each morning, you're still with me. Psalms 139:17-18 TPT

In 2021, the Lord called our family to homeschool our oldest son. It was a big leap of faith for us as I stepped away from my occupation as a Christian counselor to a stay at home with my children and homeschool my oldest. It wasn't an easy transition at first, but we saw the Lord's hand in it through many confirmations. My husband was soon after blessed with increase and recognition in the workplace, and he has continued to soar doing a job that he loves. I say all of this to show you that when you are obedient to do what God is calling you to do, you will have the grace to do it and be richly blessed. We are now finishing up with our second year of homeschooling, and it has been a wonderful experience for both myself and my son.

We have a pretty steady routine now, and always start our day in the Word of God. On this particular day that I want to share with you, we were reading Psalm 139. My son decided to make a drawing of God after reading Psalm 139 from our Bible lesson. He drew a picture of God as a great big giant man, with a crown on His head, long hair, long legs, and great big hands. He then drew a picture of the sun to the top left. He then drew two bubbles above God's head, and they both had stick figure people in them. He told me it shows that God is great and big, and always thinking of us. He said we were the people in the bubbles above God's head because we are on His mind. I couldn't hold back the tears! My son was ministering to me. This image reminded me just how special we are to God, and that He cares about every part of our lives.

There are days when we all have felt small and

insignificant, unseen by the busy world. But the truth is that there is someone who does see you. God does. You are so important to God, and He is thinking of you right now. You are on His mind. He cares for you and for what you care about. He's not distant and unaware, but present with you even as you read this. Another part of this is that sometimes we will feel afraid to step out into the deep and unknown waters God is calling us to. That was homeschool for us. But God is showing me through my son that He is with us when we take those steps of faith, and we will see the fruit of our obedience. Just as I witnessed through my son that day, and many days since.

PRAYER FOR TODAY

Lord Jesus, I trust You and Your perfect plan for my life. I trust that Your pleasant path leads me to pleasant places. I'm overwhelmed by the privileges that come with following You! I am overwhelmed by Your unchanging, unconditional love. In Your Name I pray, Amen. (Scripture reference: Psalm 16:6 TPT)

DAY 27:
LET GOD HAVE A TURN

The Lord is good to those who wait [confidently] for Him, To those who seek Him [on the authority of God's word]. Lamentations 3:25 AMP

"Let God have a turn!" shouted my oldest son as he was watching one of his favorite Christmas movies. In the movie there was a train that had lost control and was picking up speed rapidly. In my son's child-like faith, he just knew that God could stop that train and get those people to safety! Just as he was watching his movie, I happened to be in the kitchen washing dishes, rehearsing the worries and cares of the day. My mind had been running in circles about a situation that was out of my control, but when my son said that, it caused me to stop and think. This situation was out of my control entirely, but it wasn't out of God's control. This wasn't outside of His wheelhouse to solve. I had done all I could do in the natural, but it wasn't impossible for God. I needed to place my trust in God, and not in myself, to fix the issue. I needed to rest in His faithfulness.

As a Mom of three boys, resting can be hard to even imagine. I am constantly attending to their needs all day until my head hits the pillow. And then there are those times when I would hear little feet coming across the hallway in the middle of the night needing to go potty, water to drink, or for a spot in the middle of my bed. When I was pregnant with my children, the time I would feel the most movement from them was in a position of rest. Rest not only caused me to be still and relax, but it also seemed to be when my baby decided to show off! I wondered if God was showing me that there are times when He will ask me to move, but there will also be times He will ask me to be still and let Him work. That by being still, I was actually allowing God to move on my behalf. Being still is a strong position and not a weak one. Oftentimes, movement can be a distraction to us and not really make the situation any better. It doesn't mean that we just sit back and let whatever happens, happen! Instead, we choose to move more purposefully as God leads us. We are able to hear from God in the stillness. We are able to shift from worry to war in prayer. We begin to intercede for that person or situation, and call on God for help. By being still we are putting our faith to action by trusting in God. God has a way of showing us an answer to a problem that we didn't see before! I don't know about you, but I have wasted many a day worrying over things that didn't even mount up to be anything. I know we both would rather move more purposefully with God instead of spinning our wheels. I am so thankful God is showing us the ways we get off track like the train from the movie. We don't have to go full speed ahead when a problem arises. The best thing we can do is to get still before the Lord and pray, give our burden to Him, and move with purpose as He leads.

PRAYER FOR TODAY

Lord Jesus, I thank You for reminding me to slow down. I want to stay on a steady pace with You, following Your lead. I want to flow in the rhythm You have made for me, and move with purpose. In Your Name I pray, Amen.

DAY 28:
RISE UP WARRIOR

Arise [from spiritual depression to a new life], shine [be radiant with the glory and brilliance of the LORD]; for your light has come, And the glory and brilliance of the LORD has risen upon you. For in fact, darkness will cover the earth And deep darkness will cover the peoples; But the LORD will rise upon you [Jerusalem] And His glory and brilliance will be seen on you. Nations will come to your light, And kings to the brightness of your rising. Isaiah 60:1-3 AMP

It doesn't matter what season of life you may find yourself in; God is always speaking to His children. I often hear His voice the loudest through the lives of my own children. My oldest son decided that he was going to line up all his transformers on the table in the living room, and then he ran off to play with something else. As I looked down and watched what he was doing and saw those transformer action figures, I had this thought come to mind..."This is what's inside of you. A warrior!"

Just in case you don't know what toy transformers are, they look like regular cars or trucks at first but when you move their legs and arms a certain way, they transform into mighty mechanical soldiers ready for battle! It may feel that way with us sometimes when we look on the outside. We look in the mirror, and we don't see anything super special about us, but the truth is God has placed within us so much MORE! He has given us the Holy Spirit to empower us, equip us, guide us, and mold us into the image of Jesus! The Lord has given us as believers "authority [that you now possess] to tread on serpents and scorpions, and [the ability to exercise authority] over all the power of the enemy (Satan); and nothing will [in any way] harm you" (Luke 10:19 AMP). You're not going to always "feel" like you're a warrior, ready to step out and do what God has called you to do, but the beauty of it all is that you don't step out alone. You step out in faith that the Lord will meet you there, and use your obedient willing vessel to lead many into the kingdom of God and to the awakening of their identity in Christ. Let your voice for God be counted and heard! Arise, daughter of God! We are not people of hopelessness and despair; we are people of courage and confidence in our God!

We are in a time right now where evil and darkness are all around us. Yet God has called us to be a light in the darkness. It is time for the sons and daughters of God to ARISE and awaken to who they are in Christ. He has chosen YOU for such a time as this to be a giver of hope and love to a lost and hurting world around you. It's time we rise up and give the report of the Lord! Salvation has COME!! LOVE has WON!! We need to live like we know the end of the story. Jesus is coming back for us, and evil will be no more as He carries us home (Revelation 21 PARA). So from now on I want you to look at yourself differently, and see yourself as the mighty warrior God has called you to be!

PRAYER FOR TODAY

Lord Jesus, You are the greater One at work within me. Help me to arise and walk into the calling You have placed on my life. Let Your light shine through me to bring hope to a lost and hurting world. Let them see my good deeds and glorify my Father in heaven! In Your Name I pray, Amen. (Scripture references: 1 John 4:4 AMP; Matthew 5:16 NIV)

DAY 29:
DO IT AFRAID

Hezekiah put his whole trust in the GOD of Israel. There was no king quite like him, either before or after. He held fast to GOD—never loosened his grip—and obeyed to the letter everything GOD had commanded Moses. And GOD, for his part, held fast to him through all his adventures. 2 Kings 18:5-6 MSG

The Lord taught me about placing my "whole trust" in Him through my oldest son who overcame his fear of swimming in water. We were on vacation with family, and the place we were staying at had a pool. My son had been swimming a couple of times this summer but had never really felt comfortable being in the water even with his floaty on. He would always hold tightly to me when I would take him in the water and get really scared if I even tried to loosen my grip to teach him how to swim. He was perfectly content as long as his feet touched the bottom, and he was close to the steps. We even tried swimming lessons when he was younger, but it never really stuck! So I was fully prepared on this trip to be in the kiddy pool with him because that's where he feels the most comfortable. Or so I thought. As we get in the pool, I look over at my sweet boy walking down the steps to get in the "big boy" pool with his Finding Dory floaty on. He walked slowly down the steps and into the water until the water was about to his shoulders. I saw him close his eyes and start moving his arms and legs. I went over to him and asked him why he had his eyes closed, and he looked up and said, "I was praying to God that he would help me swim, and God told me I can swim if I want to!" He started moving his arms faster and kicking with the biggest grin on his face. He later told me that Jesus was teaching him how to swim, and showing him how to move his arms and kick his legs. Let me tell you, from that moment forward we had to drag him out of the pool because he wanted to swim so much! That's the goodness of our God.

My son showed me what it looks like to trust and believe that God doesn't loosen His grip on us when we step out by faith. That when we pray to Him in our time of need, our God will answer us. He is as near to us as our next thought, and He is worthy of our trust. My son hasn't yet experienced the heartache of someone making a promise to him and not keeping it. But as adults, we can count on ten fingers and ten toes how many times we've experienced this kind of disappointment. But my son just believes. He believed in that moment that God was going to be with him because his parents have always told him that truth. Now, my son is experiencing the faithfulness of God for himself. There is a scripture I think about often from 1 Kings 8:15 AMP, which says, "Blessed be the Lord, the God of Israel, who spoke with His mouth to my father David and has fulfilled it with His hand...." You will see the faithfulness of God in your life when you place your trust in Him. What He has promised in His word, which is unchanging and doesn't expire in its effectiveness, you will see Him fulfill with His hand. You will see His hand at work in your life. Our only part is to believe God is who He says He is, and walk by faith and not by sight.

PRAYER FOR TODAY

Lord Jesus, I thank You that You are fulfilling with Your hand what You promised with Your mouth! Every promise You have made will come to pass. Great is Your faithfulness! In Your Name I pray, Amen.

DAY 30:
ASSUMPTIONS CAN BE COSTLY

Abraham replied, "I thought, 'This is a godless place. They will want my wife and will kill me to get her.'" Genesis 20:11 NLT

The definition of the word assumption from the *Macmillan Dictionary* is something that you consider likely to be true, even though no one has told you directly, or even though you have no proof.[9] We have all found ourselves searching within to try and understand the world around us. What did that person mean by what they said to me? I already know this situation is going to turn out badly. I didn't get invited to that new mom group; they must not think I am a good mom. Each one of these thoughts lead us into making assumptions based on our own knowledge and reasoning. But we aren't the first ones to make assumptions.

Abraham, his wife, and family found themselves as strangers in a new land called Gerar (Genesis 20:1 NLT). When Abraham met the king of that land, Abimelech, he lied about his relationship with his wife saying she was his sister (v. 2). Taking what Abraham said as truth, King Abimelech brought Sarah to his palace (v. 2). Later that night Abimelech had a dream in which God spoke to him about Sarah and informed him that she was already married (v. 3). God warned King Abimelech that he needed to let her go back to her husband, or the consequences would be that he and all his people would die (v. 7). Abimelech quickly called for Abraham the next morning and confronted him with his deception (vv. 8-10). Abraham confessed that he had assumed King Abimelech was evil and made his decision to lie based on that assumption (vv. 11-13). This story really captured me because of how often I have made wrong assumptions about others and acted on those assumptions foolishly. Assumptions can be costly to you and to those around you. Assumptions are more often negative than positive. The enemy will often plant assumptions in our minds in hopes that we grab onto them and believe them as truth. This can be very dangerous because we can often find ourselves isolating, and adapting to negative beliefs about ourselves. It's a lose lose situation. Relationships are broken, and you end up questioning everything about yourself. What did you do? How can you change? Thankfully, God is also warning us about the harmful effects of assumptions. The solution is staying grounded in what is true. Staying grounded in what you know, and firmly planting into your heart the Word of God and what He has already said about you.

I found myself deep in an assumption one day that I was convinced had to be true. I was convinced that a person I was acquainted with did not like me for reasons unknown to me, but I had no direct proof. From my viewpoint, I was looking at how they were interacting with other people around me and felt they must like them better. It later became thoughts that something must be wrong with me. I didn't like what the situation was doing within me, so I took it to God in prayer. I got a pen and my notebook and wrote these words: "Lord, I am giving it all to you. If it's all just in my head, and what I am thinking about this person isn't true, then I am giving my mind back to you. I'm going to cling to what is good in my life, to what I know to be true today. Even so, you can transform my relationship with this person and create beauty from ashes." Nothing spectacular happened in that moment on the outside, but on the inside I was completely free of that burden and laid my assumption down. I changed my behavior as if the assumption was a lie, and was able to find joy again. I found myself even loving this person, and I treated them with an even greater kindness than before. They may have even assumed I was being unfriendly to them before, based on how I reacted to my assumption. It is so freeing when we cast our cares upon the Lord, for he cares for you (1 Peter 5:7 AMP). Let's be men and women of God who walk in truth, and don't permit assumptions to poison our minds and our relationships.

PRAYER FOR TODAY

Lord Jesus, I lay every weight at Your feet that so easily tries to entangle me. I pray that the peace of God will guard my heart and mind from the trap of assumptions. Help me to stay anchored in Your Word, and set my gaze upon You. In Your Name I pray, Amen. (Scripture references: Hebrews 12:1-2 AMP; Philippians 4:7 NIV)

DAY 31:
JUST ONE MORE TIME

Soon afterward his wife, Elizabeth, became pregnant and went into seclusion for the next five months. With joy she exclaimed, "See how kind it is of God to gaze upon me and take away the disgrace of my barrenness!" Luke 1:24-25 TPT

What do I do while I wait for my "soon"? I want to end our 31 days by encouraging you to believe God for more. To pray that the Lord would increase your faith! Elizabeth was now very late in age, and well past typical child-bearing age, but an angel of the Lord, Gabriel, appeared to her husband, Zechariah, and said that she would conceive a child. As

I read this encounter with the angel, I picture Gabriel urging Zechariah to pick up hope just one more time. Just one more time is all that it will take. I picture an in depth conversation where Zechariah explains that he has longed for a child, pleaded in prayer, and had given up on that dream. And the angel of the Lord encouraged him by saying your prayers were heard, only believe one more time, pick up hope one more time (Luke 1 PARA).

You can imagine how hard it was for both Zechariah and Elizabeth to believe one more time after praying for many years. I can understand this feeling as I am sure you can too. Being afraid of the disappointment in picking up hope again, and believing God for your miracle. I hope that by now you have learned a little more about the character of God through His Word, and it has revived your faith. That you have come to understand that God sees us, speaks to us, and works miracles in our lives. I hope that you've decided to open your heart to the possibility that God wants to work a miracle for you today. He is not too distant that He is unaware of you and your needs. He just wants your faith. Believe He is faithful to His Word just one more time. You'll come to know and appreciate that even unanswered prayers are answers from Him. He has every intention of working all things for your good. Sometimes we have to cling to the character and nature of God, who we know Him to be, in the middle of the waiting. Feast on His faithfulness just as we read from Psalm 37:3-5 (TPT). Let the times He has been faithful to you be your nourishment for today.

ONE MORE THING

In a season of doubt and confusion I heard the Lord speak these words to me: "Live in the parameters I have given you. The parameters of what I allow you to know, and trust Me when I withhold information to implore your trust. Reaching beyond the understanding I've granted invites jealousy, confusion, fear, and control to be master."

Don't let fear keep you from praying to God one more time for that prodigal child, that health need, that financial need, the desire for a child. Rest in His sovereignty, submit to His timeline, and trust Him for your breakthrough. Avoid the trap to understand your situation from your limited perspective. Pray Isaiah 55:8-9, and ask God to bring you up higher with Him and learn His thoughts (AMP). Don't stop being persistent in your prayers for heaven's intervention in your lives. Giving up is not an option. You will find all throughout the Bible the men and women of great faith making mistakes, but you won't find them giving up. They may have had moments where their faith was challenged, but they didn't give up on God and saw miracles take place. I can testify that He is faithful, and He is not just sitting back while you are in pain. He is Jehovah Shammah, the Lord is there, and He is the Lord who fights for you (Ezekiel 48:35 AMP; Exodus 14:14 AMP).

> "Keep trusting in the Lord and do what is right in his eyes. Fix your heart on the promises of God, and you will dwell in the land, feasting on his faithfulness. Find your delight and true pleasure in Yahweh, and he will give you what you desire the most. Give God the right to direct your life, and as you trust him along the way, you'll find he pulled it off perfectly!" Psalms 37:3-5 TPT

Now it's your turn to write out your story and watch God work wonders through your testimony!

LESLIE WARREN lives in Eastern North Carolina with her beloved husband, Greg, and together they have three beautiful boys. Leslie has a background in Social Work and Christian Counseling. Leslie is currently a stay-at-home mom and homeschool mom. Leslie has had the opportunity to serve her local church in various ministries, including discipleship and missions. She has a heart that is passionate to see the body of Christ awakened to their identity in Jesus and to walk in freedom.

ENDNOTES

1. Ballard, Ann. "Treasures Unseen." ©1977 Curb Word Music (ASCAP).
2. James Strong LL.D., S.T.D. The New Strong's Exhaustive Concordance Of The Bible. (Nashville, Tennessee: Thomas Nelson Publishers, 1996), 1052.
3. James Strong LL.D., S.T.D. The New Strong's Exhaustive Concordance Of The Bible. (Nashville, Tennessee: Thomas Nelson Publishers, 1996), 458.
4. James Strong LL.D., S.T.D. The New Strong's Exhaustive Concordance Of The Bible. (Nashville, Tennessee: Thomas Nelson Publishers, 1996), 326.
5. Website: Merriam-Webster. "Redeeming."

Accessed 2023. https://www.merriam-webster.com/dictionary/redeeming.
6. Website: Enduring Word. "Commentary on Matthew 11." Accessed April 11, 2023. https://enduringword.com/bible-commentary/matthew-11/.
7. Website: Merriam-Webster. "Strife." Accessed 2023. https://www.merriam-webster.com/dictionary/strife.
8. Website: Enduring Word. "Commentary on John 1." Accessed April 2023. https://enduringword.com/bible-commentary/john-1/.
9. Website: Macmillan Dictionary. "Assumption." Accessed 2023. https://tinyurl.com/hzdpwz4x

Made in the USA
Middletown, DE
09 February 2025